Jane's Journal

'The Truth Behind The Lies'

T.A. Rosewood

To my darling daughter, Jane,
Saw this notebook & thought of you - my beautiful little
butterfly.
Thought you could make it into a diary, I know how much
you used to enjoy your journal writing,
Love always, Mum. xxx

January 1st

Goodness me - Another new year!

Mum bought me this lovely notebook (she knows how much I love butterflies) so I'm going to try really hard to fill the whole year as a diary.

Thanks Mum.x

I'm so excited to see what this year brings to us all.

The kids settled back into secondary school so well in September and before we knew it, Christmas had come and gone!

And now here we are - January 1st!

I'm hoping we can get a nice long holiday this year, maybe during the summer holidays with a short break in the Easter maybe. I know the kids want to do a few theme parks so will have to fit a long weekend in for those.

Waffle waffle - lol…

Happy new year to us! xxx

January 2nd

Not much to write about tonight - everything is fine and dandy with us all.

Sarah wants to have a little meet up about the salon and a bit of a re-decorating evening. I'm so up for that!

I love her creative ideas - maybe we can get Cassie involved??

Mum brought some homemade biscuits round and we spent an hour or so chatting over a bottle of wine that one of her friends had bought her for Christmas.

She doesn't drink too much - and bless her, gets very giggly with it. Sooo love her.

Nighty night.xx

January 3rd

Made an appointment with doctor Bell so he can have a look at my lump.

Should've done it a month or so back but it's booked in now so I will just have to wait and see what he says.

Kids go back to school in a few days - will miss their voices around the house, but not their arguing LOL...

I'm back at work tomorrow.

Got some new clients lined up and I think Karl is pitching for a new project too which I must catch up with him about.

*Note to self: Make sure kids' uniforms are washed and ironed.

January 4th

Work was super busy today and it went so fast too. I couldn't wait to get home to see the kids for their last day before they are back to school.

They got the bus and met me at work so we could go straight to get pizza together with Sarah.

Karl had to work a bit later tonight but we had a nice hour chatting in the bath when he did get home.

I love my little chair in the bathroom - it's so handy for us to sit and chat together whenever we like at bathtime.

Night for now.x

January 5th

I finished work half an hour earlier today so I could pick the kids up from school.

They had a lovely first day back and it was great to hear about all the new projects they have coming up as well as getting to choose their options for GCSE year.

Crikey! How quick has that come round.

Another busy few days coming up for all of us including mum who has another club to go to - I don't know how she fits them all in.

Note to self: Organise a shopping trip with mum - been too long. :)

Night.x

January 6th

I went with mum this afternoon to take some flowers to pops. We always get him some fresh ones - he loved his flowers so much.

Had a good chat with mum while we sat there about her maybe meeting someone - she was having none of it. Just laughed the idea off but I do wish she would have a companion at least.

I know she's not lonely because of how many friends and clubs she has but to have someone to enjoy all that with and to love her again would be so lovely to see - she deserves it.

I'll keep my fingers crossed that she may change her mind one day. I'll keep trying to convince her.

Sleepy tonight so signing off early.xxx

January 7th

I had my appointment with the doctors today but I cancelled it. I don't want to bother him with it and, to be honest, I've just got too much on this week.

I know I shouldn't have cancelled and just gone to get it checked but it's nothing to worry about - just the scar tissue. :/

Karl also said I should've gone, but he knows when I've made my mind up, so, that's that.

I will re-book in a few weeks when life isn't so hectic.

The kids went back to school and all is good so far!

Xmas decs will come down this weekend :(booooo - if only Christmas lasted all year. lol.

xx

January 9th

Oops, missed a few days.

Anyway, the weekend flew by as always and that's Christmas done for another year. :(

I always feel a bit sad when the decs are all packed away. There's always a bauble or two that get broken as the tree gets taken down.

I think this coming Christmas, I'll get a new set, maybe in a new colour? Maybe go for a white theme with a hint of silver.?? So many choices...

I'd love to get a set of reindeer for the front garden too - they can sit on the grass next to the blow up Santa. LOL....Karl loves him... :)

Crazy Christmas lady, Yep, that's me! :)

Sarah and mum came over for dinner - we all had fun and teased Sarah about getting a new boy-friend but she was having none of it. I get the impression, she'd rather have dogs. Bless her.

Karl's doing some extra work in the study - he's been on the phone for ages with his new temp,

Harriet…

I always get a bit on edge when these young beautiful temps are taken on at his work - no idea why, I don't have anything to worry about with Karl.

Guess it's an age thing - I'm not getting any younger am I.

But he loves me and I love him.x

Doing a bit of reading on my kindle tonight before sleep, hoping he comes to bed soon.

Night. xx

January 10th

Karl and I ended up having an argument last night - we've not done that for months.

It was horrible and over something so stupid. :(

Why would I even think he would fancy someone else in his office too - overthinking the hot new blonde temp I guess.

Urghhh....I don't know what is wrong with me.

Sometimes I wonder if it's this lump issue causing me to doubt how he feels about me, causing me to be self conscious that I'm not perfect - that's silly though as he says it doesn't bother him, he says he can't feel it when I have said anything or pointed it out to him.

I just hope the kids didn't hear us - I don't want them to worry about us.
We made up this afternoon by text and promised we would talk it over next time - well, hopefully there won't be a next time anytime soon - I hate not talking to him.

I'm not usually a jealous person but just got aggravated when he kept talking about her when he did eventually come to bed.

Sometimes I wish we had gone into the same business so we could have worked together but, then again, maybe that's not such a good idea.

It's nice that we have our own careers - gives us something to chat about at night.

I'll get him a little something tomorrow to say sorry or maybe we could arrange a night out - just the two of us...?

:(

January 11th

It seems like a week for arguing. :(

Rob had a fight at school so we got a phone call from the head. All over football teams, Boys!

I got Karl his favourite bottle of red to make up for the other night - although he said he'd forgotten all about it - men!

LOL. xx

Cassie wants to start the whole shaving legs, arm-pits malarkey, she's growing up way too fast and it's scary but I remember it well. Will have to buy some bits.

Work was fine so not much else to write tonight.

Bye for now.x

January 13th

So much for writing every day, I seem to keep forgetting at nights, being too tired and busy with everything else I suppose.

I've also been thinking about re-booking my doctor's appointment but again, I keep talking myself out of it, so another week has gone and it's not been checked out. Will look at days next week.

I thought a lot about pops today - there was a documentary on TV about cancer and how quickly it can take hold of people.

Well, that was certainly true for pops. I miss him...

I miss you pops.

xx

January 28th

Mum's Birthday...x

Another load of days missing in this...

Anyway, I spent the afternoon with mum today - we went into Cambridge and I treated her to a High Tea for her birthday. She loves a bit of posh dining does mum.

I think she enjoyed it although she seemed a bit down - she's been thinking about pops a lot, one of her friends has just been diagnosed with lung cancer and I think it's just brought the memories flooding back, bless her.

I told her to come over to ours for dinner but she insisted she would be fine and was meeting up with Rita from bridge club (I think it was that club anyway, she has so many).

I love her dearly but she's one independent, strong woman and I'm so proud of her. Hope she's okay tonight.
Love you mum..xxx

February 1st

I've been thinking about what to do for the twins' birthdays - it's only a few weeks and we've not really talked about it.

Becoming teenagers is a big deal so maybe they want to do something big.

Should've really asked them a bit earlier in case they want a big party. Maybe we can have a chat tomorrow night with Karl.

Can't believe they will be 13 already.

Sarah has arranged to take them and me to Yarmouth Pleasure beach - it will be nice for the four of us to take some time out and have some crazy fun like that.

Sarah and I went there for my 15th birthday, such fun memories of that day.

Sugary donuts, chips on the beach and lashings of icecreams to die for! yum....

My parents took us for the weekend and we had such a blast - I wonder if it's changed much since then. probably.

Anyway, night for now, Jane.x

February 3rd

We talked to the kids about their big birthday but didn't get very far with any plans.

None of them could really think of anything to do other than getting pizza and maybe a trip to the cinema or crazy golf.

Maybe they just need a few days to have a think about what to do? Won't push them, they are turning into teenagers after all.

I suppose they could just have a pizza night and a friend over maybe?

I'll leave it to them to let me know.

Not much else happening otherwise.

Night. J.x

February 14th

Valentines Day xxx <3 <3 <3

Oops....Another few weeks since I wrote in this - I was really hoping to make this year when I could write every day but hey ho - life takes over, things get busy.

My diaries used to be full to the brim when I was a teenager - seemed to have too much to say back then..or maybe just more time on my hands to write stuff, who knows.

I will try a bit harder...again.

Writing before work just to make sure I fit something in.

Gave Karl his Valentine's card this morning before he rushed off to work.

I tried to get up a bit earlier to make him breakfast in bed but he had already gotten up for a run. Fitness freak. :)

Off to work now, will maybe write something tonight before bed.

Byeeee.x
J.xx

February 15th

Last night was so lovely.

Karl came home with a big bunch of red roses and a bottle of my fav sparkly cava for Valentine's Day - he's such a romantic at times.

We didn't go out, I was too tired, so instead, we ordered an Indian and ate outside on the patio - it was such a warm evening for February. Lovely.

Robbie got a little card posted through the door, with just a question mark in it which Cass thought was hilarious. He just shrugged it off - I don't think boys think the same as girls when it comes to this sort of thing.

Bless him for having a little admirer. He is such a handsome boy though, if I do say so myself...I'm not going to be surprised if he gets even more over the next few years. Any girl would be lucky to have him as their boyfriend - and husband some-day...eek...imagine that!

I still haven't managed to make my doctor's appointment - urghhh, that's a few months now - I want to but don't want to, if that makes sense.

I felt it in the shower this morning and I think it's got smaller anyway now so I will leave it and see how it goes over the next few months.

Bath and Bed now...

xxx

February 21st

Twins birthday - 13..!!!

So there it is, our little babies are now officially teenagers! Wow...

They didn't want to do anything which was surprising, so we just had a small party at home with Sarah and mum.

More of a gathering of family really I guess.

Mum made them a gorgeous cake each - I honestly don't know where she found the time but they tasted yummy and looked so beautiful. She has such a talent for cake making and the kids loved them.

I'll have to try and stick some pics in here.

*Note to self: Print off the cake pics.

They both had a friend come over later for sleepovers in the garden though.

After we had dinner, the tent malarkey started.
It was hilarious watching Karl, Rob and his friend

trying to get both the tents up.

I think maybe Karl had one too many beers this afternoon. LOL…

Cass and her friend just entertained themselves painting their nails in the kitchen while they waited for their tent to be finished. :)

Sarah stayed to help with the clearing up and we chatted again about the salon and the fact that she hadn't had a date for a few months. Turns out she has been seeing someone but knows it's nothing serious.

She's such a funny one but so lovely too. I hope she finds the right one soon, she deserves to be happy and share her beautiful life with someone special.

Can still hear the kids giggling in the garden, not much sleep going on here tonight I guess…

Night night.x
xx

February 22nd

So, the sleepovers went okay in the end. I think it was about 3am by the time the giggling and chatting stopped but hey ho, they all had fun.

I used to love having sleepovers, Sarah stayed over so much at mine before she had to go and live with her aunt for a year.

She changed after that - not in a bad way at all but just, oh I don't know - grew up a bit I suppose.

She had to take care of her aunt so I guess that would make you grow up all of a sudden.

Anyway, another busy week so I will try and write in here when I can. (Not promising though, lol) :)

Byeeeee...xxx
Jane.xxx

March 3rd

Karl's Birthday!!

I did say I wouldn't promise to write...oh dear, what am I like. Another few weeks have flown by again...

Anyway...It was my man's birthday.

So tonight we went out for dinner for his birthday. Just a little Indian at one of his fav restaurants and then a nice walk through town afterwards.

It's the simple things :) but Cambridge is such a beautiful city with the most amazing buildings.

I bought him a couple of new shirts - he didn't want anything but I did notice a few weeks back that a few of his shirts were getting a bit tatty.

What is it with men and wearing shirts to death?

When we got home, he spent some time with the kids, playing some new footy game with Rob and then chatting to Cassie about all things painting and arty. I took that time to have a little bubble bath.

Once the kids were asleep and he had a shower, I took advantage of him...oops...heehee, best say no more in here.

All in all - a lovely birthday for him I think and time well spent together. Xxx

Jane.xx

March 5th

Only missed a few days writing - maybe I'm getting better at this diary lark again, we'll see. Hee hee.

Anyway, update of the little lumpy loo.

I felt for it again while I had a shower this morning and I don't know what to do really. It seems like it's moved or got smaller so maybe massaging it at night is doing the job - dispersing the scar tissue finally.

I read somewhere that daily massaging can help so I've been giving that a go for a week or two now.

Not going to bother the doctor with it for now. Sure it will be gone in a few months.

Work was soooo quiet today at work - hope it picks up soon, there's only so much re-organising of files you can do when bored.

Carol said to go early so I popped in to see Sarah on the way home - took her a nice bucksie and her favourite choccy cookie.

We discussed trying to get a girls night again but may have to be for her birthday now as she has so much on with the salon and training some new girls. I love her success with it and love helping her with new ideas.

Fajitas for dinner tonight so gonna crack on with it.

Speak soon..
J.x

March 15th

I'm not doing so well at this diary lark am I...???

Another ten days gone and no writing...

I just keep forgetting to spend those all import-ant five minutes per evening just to get something written in here. Then sometimes I can't seem to stop writing. Madness.

I guess life just gets busy but hey, as a quick catch up (with nothing really exciting), work's been fine, little bit quiet still, kids have been good - getting on at school and making new friends.

Karl is very busy with work stuff and doing a bit of painting in the hallway.

Sarah is Sarah..lol...Crazy but beautiful.

Mum - always a busy bee with clubs, friends and keeping her house and garden lovely as ever.

Life is GOOD!!! :)

March 21st

I've been thinking about my upcoming birthday next month - I can't believe I'm going to be 39 already.

The last few years seem to have flown past so quickly but mum told me once you get a job, kids, husband and a house to keep - before you know it, life creeps by, and she was so right - she's always right.

It's such a busy start to the year with birthdays and celebrations.

First Mums' birthday, then the twins, then Karls', mine then Sarahs' and lastly our wedding anniversary. At least the last half of the year, we get a little break from birthdays and such.

I do love a good celebration though and giving presents is something I enjoy. I want to get Sarah something special for next year - we both turn 40 so maybe we could go away or something.

*Note to self: Have a chat with Sarah regarding the big 40 event. Lol.

Anyway, back to this year (before I turn really old), I'm going to ask Karl if we can just keep it a bit low key, dinner, bowling or cinema - I'd rather spend it with him and the kids, Sarah and mum. I mean the bog party can be next year - maybe we should have a joint party..mmm, brain is working overtime to-night.

Kids have started working on exam stuff at school - that's crazy and scary too but sure they'll cope fine with it.

Might need to discuss extra tutoring in maths for Cass maybe? Or I might just spend an hour every other evening with her - yes, that might be better for her.

Nighty night...x

March 24th

So I only missed a few days but still - not really good enough is it - I won't have any memories to look back on for this year if I don't step it up a bit more with the writing so come on Mrs W...write more.

Mum's coming over tomorrow to help Cassie with some baking for a school fundraiser - will be nice to see them working together.

*Note to self: get cake ingredients after work.

Lump...It's still hanging around but it's better - I think anyway, so, not making an appointment just yet.

It'll be fine. :)

Karl worked late again last night - I don't like it much especially with the gorgeous new girls that they seem to be having work there lately - feeling a little insecure again lately - must try and stop that, don't want another row with him about something stupid like being that annoying jealous wife.

Anyway, I finally got round to printing out the

twins' cakes that mum made for their birthdays - only a month on.

Lol, but I've decided to put them in a frame with one of the pics Sarah took instead of putting them in here. She managed to capture the twins blowing the candles out together - a great photo.

Soooo beautiful…

March 27th

So it's nearly my birthday - eek.

Decided to just do dinner and bowling so booked that all in this afternoon.

Not much else going on - the usual footy training for Robbie and dancing classes for Cassie.

Karl has to find another member of staff to cover for someone going on maternity leave.

Work is picking up - new client today for me.

All good with little lumpy in my bumpy...fingers crossed it stays that way - not worrying.

April 7th

MY BIRTHDAY!!

Ooops….ten days missed, hey ho.

So I turned 39 today. God, it's the big one next year!

We went out for dinner and bowling afterwards - it was so much fun.

Cassie painted me a beautiful picture of a butterfly and Rob bought me some of my favourite perfume.

Sarah got me a new mug for work which says 'Crazy book lady' on it and mum got me a new cooking apron - always the practical one she is. Xxx

It's been a lovely birthday and there was even talk of a big 40 birthday party for next year! 40.!!

Seriously, how did that even happen?
Oh well, I have a year to get used to that!!

LOL…

New Netflix series started, wine poured.

Nighty night. xxx

April 9th

A package came yesterday but it was addressed to Karl so I left it for him.

At first, I got a bit suspicious as he didn't open it straight away and just took it straight upstairs. He's normally one to rip open packages as soon as they drop on the doormat.

Then when we went to bed, he surprised me with a gorgeous new negligee (late birthday arrival).

It was laid out on the bed with rose petals around it - he's such a sweetie sometimes and I didn't have a clue that he'd done all that so it was even more special.

Anyway, needless to say, it didn't stay on the bed for too long!!! :)

Beautiful evening - that's all I'm saying. <3

Night. Xx

April 16th

Again, here I am saying sorry to this diary for missing another week or so of writing - grrr.

It's just so busy and then at night all I want to do is spend time with Karl and the children.

We know from losing pops that time just slips away, life is so short and we have to make the most of this time.

Why am I even making excuses or writing this...hahaha....maybe I'm losing my mind a bit - old age. LOL...

Anyway, off to sit with my gorgeous husband to finish off that new series we started.

Speak soon, hopefully.

J.xxx

May 1st

Got in touch with a few of the girls today while at work to try and sort something for Sarah's birthday.

We decided to book a meal together in Cambridge instead of doing London this year. Think we are all getting too old for that.

Anyway, I've ordered her a few bits to make sure they are here in time and I must remember to grab some nice wrapping paper this weekend.

*Note to self: Get wrapping paper and ribbon.

Watched a movie tonight with the twins - Karl had to work late so I treated them to pizza and popcorn.

Update on lump: I had a shower just now and it seems it is staying around - I might book that appointment after all - just to make sure.

I don't want to panic about it and worry anyone so will call them on my lunch break in next few days.

Tiring day today so off for an early night, hope Karl isn't too long.

Nighty night.x

May 7th

It seems I am dithering once again with this and missed another week - last month I only managed three days I think!

I have been busy with work stuff and trying to help the children with their new subjects and all the projects and work they have to get prepared.

Diary will have to be in the backburner for the next few weeks maybe.

I'll try and update more.

I still haven't made the doctor's appointment either - do I need to? Probably not...it'll be fine.

Really looking forward to Sarah's birthday do now - she will be so surprised I've kept it a secret.

YAY...XX

May 15th

SARAH'S B/D :)

So, tonight was such fun.

The girls - together again.

Sarah was so shocked that we had managed to keep it from her, especially me I think - I usually tell her everything.

The meal was delicious and afterwards, we went to a nightclub. (Interesting) :)

I think I'm getting too old for this club malarkey. Lol.

We had a fab time anyway and by the end of the night Abbie had pulled herself an admirer and a phone number or two I think...Good on her. Since her boyfriend's terrible bike accident, she's not been able to date for some time. Such a sad thing to happen to such a young guy - she deserves to be happy again, bless her. x

Karl came and picked us up - Sarah was a little

worse for it so she's in the spare room sleeping it off.

I can't believe how much we used to go to clubs when we were younger - it's exhausting now. Lol.

Anyway, that's it for birthdays for a while now, phew!

Off for some cuddles now with my man...

Night..xx

May 22nd

ANNIVERSARY TIME!

Today was our wedding anniversary - I can't believe we have been married for 19 years now - it's the big one next year along with my big birthday too - but let's not discuss that one just yet (not ready for the big 4.0.)

Karl bought me another new negligee, some perfume, flowers, chocolates and a new photo frame for the mantle piece.

Will be trying out the negligee a bit later.

I got him some new slippers (trying to encourage him to wear them around the house), a new jacket for when he's at footy training with Robbie and a new wallet.

We're off to dinner soon so writing this up quickly while he has a shower - I know we will be too busy to write later…:) well I hope so anyhow.

Night for tonight.

J.x

May 23rd

We had a lovely anniversary - it really was special.

Mum came over to sit with the kids for a change from Sarah - she had another date which is exciting.

The meal was really nice and time with my man was as always - wonderful.

Unfortunately, when we got home, Cassie had been throwing up - she thinks she had something dodgy from the swimming pool cafe - although I think it may be heat stroke as it's been crazy hot these past few days - weird for May but I think that may be the case.

Night.
x

June 9th

I can't believe we are halfway through this year already.

Where does the time go?

It's flying by so fast already - scary really :/

I've completely neglected this notebook/diary.

Jeez - all my good intentions of keeping one from the 1st of Jan went down the spout - sorry about that.

I promise to try harder from now on.

It will soon be the summer holidays again, the kids will be off school (which we love), and Sarah will be ultra busy getting everyone summer ready with their beauty treatments.

*Note to self: book eyebrows in for next week.

I must remember to start looking at holiday ideas with Karl and the kids at some point.

Sarah mentioned Mexico but I think that's a little bit exotic for the children at their age. I don't think they are quite old enough to appreciate the beauty of Mexico just yet so maybe in a few years time.

Karl fancies Barbados but maybe for our second honeymoon or something.

As much as we love a family holiday, it would be nice to have a week away just the two of us somewhere romantic like that.

*Note to self: grab some holiday brochures from town.

Work this week is going to be super busy. New clients always bring a bit of a buzz to the office.
Tomorrow, we have our charity breast cancer awareness day so that's going to be a bit of a different day at work.

Carol has been amazing at getting it all organised, she's so funny sometimes juggling so much that's going on. It seems like she never stops working and always has her phone glued to her ear practically.

I guess some might say that about me these days too, they are the norm and almost a lifeline for everyone. I don't know what I'd do without it to be fair.

Maybe this diary should be written in there instead - have to look to see if there are any diary apps maybe, although I do love a good pen and paper, and this is such a lovely notepad from mum, seems a shame not to use it for this type of thing - just gotta try harder to write in it more.

Anyway...
Cassie and I have been busy making little pink ribbon badges to sell to all the staff and any visitors that come into the office on the day. They are so pretty.

It's been so lovely spending time with her doing this type of thing. We chatted about pops and what type of cancer he had, but also talked about breast cancer and she was asking so many questions. I hope I managed to answer them okay.

She said she wanted the little badges to be perfect. So sweet & so creative - and as it turns out, a perfectionist. So much like her dad in that way.

She has done most of the work with them - I didn't have to do much really, more just passing her what she needed to be fair. Her little fingers work so much quicker than mine do or did at her age.

I used to love getting involved helping pops with things around the house and garden but he was the practical one and me, well I was more the side-kick helper. LOL...:)

I wonder sometimes if she may go into something in fashion or Art with all the creations she comes out in from her room at times.

She seems to have an eye for creating a style with

anything.

She's growing up way too fast now, they both are actually.

Their nursery days seem like a lifetime ago, and now they are at highschool, it's going to fly even quicker I'm pretty sure of that.

Robbie has even set up his own after school group to teach students about gaming, that's pretty cool.

Sooo proud of them both :)

Karl is excited about a new work project, it's nice to see him pumped up and most of all keeping him busy.
I love him so much. xx

Signing off now to have a chilled glass of wine in the garden with my love.

Let's see what this week brings our little family.
x

June 10th

Today turned out to be a bit more interesting than I thought it would be.

At work, I had my check up with the nurses, who I might add, were soooo lovely and friendly.

I felt slightly nervous but they seemed to have a way of making everyone feel so much more relaxed.

The mammogram scan was in this massive lorry that took up most of the front grounds but it wasn't too bad actually. More uncomfortable than painful and the squishy boob machine was soooo cold, but again, the nurses were lovely about it all.

I wouldn't want to do that job every day for sure. They are doing amazing things and saving people's lives by doing that job.

Incredible work ladies - my hat comes off to you all. :)

I asked them to have a quick look at the lump I keep feeling just under my left boob.

Hopefully, this little lump issue I have will be sorted soon and I can then stop thinking about it.

I suppose I should've got it looked at before now but it's just some silly scar tissue which I believe can just be removed with a minor operation I think. Or maybe I can have it lasered out or something??

Pretty convinced the breast reduction must have caused it. I didn't manage to get enough drainage massages afterwards so the scar tissue must have gathered quicker.

I've read about people having this sort of thing after operations. I have a bit where the c-section was done. I guess it's trauma to the body like that. I don't know - I'm no doctor I suppose. :/

It's been a good few months, maybe more but I'm not a fan of going to the doctors at the best of times. I've spent too much time there over the past few years with pops and all that worry and upset. I tend to self diagnose and then just buy over the counter medicine if and when I need it although, thinking about it, I don't really get poorly that often so hey ho...! lol

Anyway, I've had my check and donated to the fabulous cause so just have to wait and see what comes back now.
Sure it'll be all fine and dandy. :)

There's a girl in the office who hasn't got much in the boob department and she was so funny after her appointment, joking about not being able to get them into the jaws of the machine, (her words not mine), bless her. Xx

I'm okay with my chest size now even though they developed quite early on, which at the time I found annoying.

The reduction just helped with the back ache from the boobs but it's only taken me down a size so they are manageable now - what am I talking about here - BOOBS!!

LOL...x

Anyway, I just need this lump gone now and I can forget about it all finally and love my boobies again.

This afternoon seemed to fly by, busy as per normal with the new clients emailing and signing up with us. It's been a bit tense lately with client numbers wavering but I'm sure it'll pick up soon. Carol has a way of drawing people to the company.

The kids had some tests at school.

Robbie was a little worried this morning but I'm sure he worries more than he needs to. He doesn't much like tests, who does? But I'm sure they'll both be fine.

I love seeing how they are growing up but it seems to be flying by so quickly as the years go on.
I wonder sometimes, what they'll be like as little adults.

I'm so excited to see them excel in what they choose to do and even more excited to see them marry and have their own children one day in the distant future - the very distant future! I'm not ready to be a grandma for a while yet. :)

Imagine it! Me and Karl Grandparents - wow, such a wonderful thought of times to come.

I'd love for them to travel a bit first before settling down.

I wish I had seen a bit more of the world before the twins came along but I wouldn't change anything - not one little bitty bit. They are my life. The four of us are complete and it's fabulous.

Home time: We all had a lovely meal together this evening. I made one of our fav meals - fajitas which were quickly demolished.
I really need to arrange a date night with Karl soon though, it seems like months since we went out, just the two of us.

We used to go out so much when we started dating, trying all different types of food cuisine, but it's so cool now - we love spending time together and experiencing new food places as a family when we can.

I must remember to tell them about that new Turkish place on the high street that Sarah went to the other evening. She said Karl would love it…and she is rarely wrong about food and my husband. lol.x

*Note to self…get a date night booked in asap.

Night for now.
J x

June 11th

So this morning, I had an unexpected phone call. :/

Paula from the breast clinic rang me about my screening results, so I popped by to see them at lunch time.

I just told Carol it was to the opticians, so she didn't worry. She always tends to stress out if she knows someone has a doctor's appointment suddenly, especially at short notice.

No need for her to know about me though - I'm always fine and dandy. :)

I had to walk there as I got the bus to work so I could catch up on a book I had downloaded a few weeks back on my kindle. Another romance novel that I had heard about from mum and her book club.

Turns out, I didn't get that chance to catch up after the clinic called me though. I felt a bit anxious about it but, after speaking to Paula on the phone, she helped me to chill out a bit. She is so nice, so friendly and helpful.

I guess you have to be that way in that type of job. x

The place was absolutely beautiful. Such a gorgeous old building in the middle of the city and cared for and maintained perfectly.

The flower displays inside and out were just - well, stunning. (I wish the flowers in our garden would look like that). I guess if I spent more time out there they might, or if pops were still around, he'd make sure they bloomed...Hey ho...

Anywho...after a chat with the doctor and to be on the safe side, they wanted to look into it a bit further.

I had to call the office to say I'd be late back - I do hate lying to people but I also hate people worrying about things when it's just not necessary so I forgive myself this time LOL...x :)

Had a few more tests including another round of hefty boob squashing which felt a bit more painful than the other day's squashing episode. Bruised maybe???

The tests and all that should be back in a few days time so will have to just wait for now.

Paula was great, again, really reassuring and the doctor was lovely too. Very professional and so smart.

I'm just hoping that they will refer me to get this

horrid hard scar tissue fixed, removed or some-thing done about it.

I hate to think that Karl can feel it. :(

He doesn't mind, he's told me hundreds of times not to worry about it, but I don't like it and it has to go.

I'm sort of glad that this awareness day has hap-pened as it has now means that I've got it looked at by professionals, should've done it ages ago but hey, busy lives and all that jazz!.

Life goes by so quickly these days it seems I don't get a chance to do a lot of stuff.

Anyway, fingers crossed for some good news on that soon!

Karl rang while I was in there and stupidly, I lied to him. Well I guess I didn't lie, I just didn't tell him exactly where I was. That's different to fibbing isn't it?

I didn't see the point in explaining where I was, it'll all be fixed soon and no-one will be the wiser to worry about me.

*Note to self: turn phone OFF not just to silent when somewhere I don't want to have to explain!

On a sadder note: I thought about pops A LOT after being at the clinic. There were so many posters and leaflets around the place that it just brought back the memories of him being so poorly.

He was taken away from us too soon, way too soon and I hate that blasted cancer for it. I HATE it with a passion. grrrr

It's so unfair that his chance to be the grandad that he was so excited to be was cut short.

God how I wish he was here to see the twins growing up now. To see him play in his garden with them. :(

He used to love having them sitting in their pram next to him while he explained all his flowers and plants, and what slugs and snails were useful for.

They were asleep most of the time which was funny but he still chatted away. Me and mum used to have a giggle at him through the kitchen window.

Grrrrr....

I miss him so much - I miss you pops. :(xx
And breathe!!!

But hey, some good news: Perry the postie had news to spread about the office! Yay. x

He and his lady are expecting a baby in mid December. What a lovely early Christmas present for him and his family. It's due on his birthday too. We are all so happy for him, he's such a fun guy.

I must remember to put the due date in this diary and maybe get a congrats card for him so we can all sign it at work. Was it the 15th or 16th..??

I think it will be the first baby born for the office lot this year. Don't know of anyone else pregnant as yet.

Definitely not me, that's for sure!

I think I've done my part on that front. Lol.

Maybe we can give him a nice baby shower, and invite his lady in. His lady...lol...Emily. x

Carol may have already made plans for this I suppose.??

*Note to self: ask Carol about the baby shower and get a card.

All the baby chatting made me think about how excited we were when we got pregnant.

I knew at first glance when I met Karl all those years ago at the fancy dress party, I knew he was the one I wanted to have children with.

Wow, that party - his Elvis impressions were hilarious and the suit! :) So funny.

Those days were so much fun and carefree for us and we couldn't wait to settle down and have children together although we never imagined having two at once. Twins! Never expected that!

We got the perfect pair though, Robbie and Cassie born just a few minutes apart, man I love them.

I thought of how Mum and dad were over the moon to find out they were going to be grandparents to twins.

I remember mum nearly fainting with joy and pops had an extra shot of scotch to calm his nerves and excitement. Lol.

Smiling to myself like a Cheshire cat right now, at the amazingly great memories our babies have given us already.

Off to dream of flowers and babies now. Lol.

Goodnight dear diary. x

June 12th

Met Sarah for lunch today, she's been telling me all about her new treatments that she's got coming up in the salon - can't wait to try them all out. I'm usually her guinea pig but I don't mind that. Gets me a bit of pamper time with her.

I might start taking Cassie for the ones that she is old enough to have anyway.
She would love them all I'm sure but may have to wait to experience the pain of waxing, bless her.

I have suggested to Sarah that she create a spa package for her customers - she loves the idea so we will have to chat about that maybe at the weekend or next time she's round for a girls night.

She did make me laugh today. She rang me to tell me about some woman who was really rude to her at work. Something about being over priced for her lash treatments but I tried to explain to her not to worry about it and try to laugh it off. She just said I was 'too nice' but it's just me and how I am I guess. I told her life is too short to worry about people like that and her prices are fair for the work she does and the products she uses on her clients.

Maybe I am too nice sometimes, it's something people tend to say about me, but I try to see the good in things and situations unless they are really bad obviously.

Why be unkind, there's enough sadness and un-kindness in the world?

Sarah is so funny with the comments she can make about people, I know she means no harm, she wouldn't be nasty to anyone on purpose and any situation is forgotten within minutes, then she's back to the fun and crazy Sarah that we all love. My bestest friend in the world ever.

Mum took me shopping, she was looking for a new selection of books for her book club to start read-ing for next month.

We popped into some charity shops and got some really good bargains from some best selling au-thors so mum was well chuffed.

She's so amazing the way she keeps herself so busy and goes to all these clubs. She has made so many new friends since pops left us and it's down to all these things she attends.

The book club was her idea and she loves it.

I'm glad for her.

Maybe she could look in our little box room for

some more, must remember to ask her if she'd like to choose a few for the following month.

*Note to self: ask mum about books.

She does make me giggle with her loud outfits but I love her dearly and wouldn't want her to be any different. Pops would be so proud of her too.

I know she misses him every day as we all do. Her visits to his grave keeps her going. I must go and see him myself again soon, I'll take him some of his favourite flowers maybe.

Anyway, signing off now, a busy few days are coming with the big meeting at work.

Night.x

June 13th

Today started bloody awful and then got even worse.

After the news the clinic gave me this afternoon, I'm struggling to write down my feelings and the shock I now feel.

I've been trying to get my head round what has just happened and to be honest, I still don't know how I feel or what the hell I am going to do.

I have no idea how Karl will react or feel about this either, god he can't find out, not yet. I can't even bring myself to think about telling him so all I can do for now is put it down in writing here, to try and help me decide what to do in my own mind first before I tackle anyone else and see their sadness and worry overflowing.

I've got to hide this diary now - I can't have anyone find it and read what's going on - not just yet. :(

This has come as such a shock and so much so that I bloody fainted when they told me the news. Right there in the clinic where I thought my pain in the butt little bit of poxy scar tissue would be sorted out.

How embarrassing! ;/

I'm not a fainter usually, I can't even remember ever fainting before this, even at the sight of blood or getting too hot. No, I cannot recall that ever happening in my life.

What an idiot!

Nurse Paula and doctor Ramsey were incredible, so friendly and understanding of me and the whole situation. I hope they can help me figure this shit out. I'm totally devastated at the moment and I don't even have the words to describe how much.

Not Cancer, not again...not me... :(

After I left the clinic, I went to see pops. I don't know why but something led me there and I actually sobbed at his graveside. The reality hit me, of the fact that I will be with him soon.

Dead, buried, no more.

Oh my god, this is killing me inside already.

I spoke to him like he was actually sitting there with me, just like I used to chat to him on his favourite garden bench, before he was taken away from me by this bloody c-word nightmare.

I felt like my heart was breaking all over again but

selfishly for myself this time and what I was going to be putting my family through, again. Bloody again.

Damn you Cancer, damn you. :(

The weird thing was, whilst I was blubbering to pops, and feeling like a complete fool, I met someone.

His name is James and he was visiting his mum's grave, cancer took her away too. What a coincidence.

I felt like a total mess, I looked like a total mess but he was so nice calming me down and so easy to talk to.

We sat on this wooden bench under the cherry blossom trees and chatted for like an hour or something.

Not all about the news but about each other mainly, I told him about Karl and the twins.
He must've thought I was a complete wreck, the state I was in, how embarrassing.

He's been through the mill a bit during his short life, his wife gave him a nice shock of leaving him for another woman but he seems to be coping okay with it all, maybe...I'm no psychiatrist, but he sees the funny side of it so that's one way of coping I suppose.

*Note to self: ask James more about his life.

I'm looking forward to seeing him again and this time, I won't cry, I won't sob.

He doesn't need that constant negativity with what he's gone through. How he's got through all that I don't know...but he's agreed to meet me again tomorrow so I'm hoping he can help me to make a decision or at least just listen. He said he's good at that and I feel I've made a friend in him. Does that sound weird so soon, should I be a bit careful? He's a stranger after all???

At the minute, I feel like I can't talk to anyone here, at home, especially Karl, even Sarah and couldn't possibly tell mum right now.

She doesn't need to hear that bloody C word again so soon.

I lied to Karl when I got home about why my eyes were in such a state, he seemed to believe me though, what is it with me lying to people these last few days.

I can't let them know the truth just yet, I just can't do it to them. I see the sadness already without even saying a thing, without anyone even knowing what's going on, that doesn't even make sense, I'm not making sense, this whole situation doesn't make sense. Urghhhh. :(

Karl was downstairs making dinner and I was sitting here wondering if my hair will fall out, when I'm going to die, crazy thoughts like that, and it's breaking my heart. I want to shout and scream but I have to stay strong, I can't lose it. I mustn't lose it, for everyone's sake at the minute.

What the hell am I going to do?

How the hell am I going to deal with this?

*Note to self: stop blubbering and think, think, think! :(x

June 14th

I've booked the day off work, I want to go back and see the doctor. I was only going to take the morning off but Carol said to take the day so I did, quite happily actually to be fair.

I don't think I've got the strength to deal with work stuff today.

At least I'll have the weekend to get my head around things, maybe just a little bit more.

Going to see what they say at the clinic, I have to fight this like pops tried to.

I just have to be here for as long as possible.

I'm not going to let it take me until I'm ready.

You won't take me Cancer until I say it's time.!!!

*Note to self: apologise for fainting.

Update:
So, I went back to the clinic – they were amazing about everything and I'm getting started with chemo on Monday afternoon. They've arranged the sessions after work so no-one has to know. I've

got some tablets to start me off. I'm hoping they don't make me feel too sick.

I popped by to see James quickly.
He was great, once again. He seems to know what to say at just the right moment. How lucky I am to have found him just at the right time too.

*Note to self: Try and enjoy the weekend now with Karl and the kids.

*Another note to self: Ask Sarah to pop round for a glass or two of wine. :)

xxx J xxx

June 15th

Today we had a chill day in the garden. I have tried so hard not to think of what begins on Monday but it's so hard.

The weather was beautiful so after Cassie had her dance class and Robbie was back from football, Karl lit the BBQ and we set up the badminton net in the garden.

Watching Karl and the kids jumping around playing hit me hard and I had to go in for a moment, pretending, or more, lying to them saying I'd got something in my eye.

Jesus!

This feels like I'm the star in my own crazy film or something.

Why can't I just sit down and talk to them, tell them this awful news.

Why? Why?...

Because it will make them all sad, they will hurt like I'm hurting, they will cry, they may even get angry...I just don't know.

For now, this has to stay with me, this is my secret until I know how to deal with it myself. Learn how to accept what's happening to me and what will happen to my family when they do know the truth!

I can't tell them, not yet. :(

*Note to self: Just enjoy my family.

Try and keep strong...

Jane.x

June 16th

Sarah came over today and we went over her spa package stuff for the salon. It was so nice seeing her smiling and excited about it all and gave me time out of my own thoughts and fears!

Cassie helped with the leaflet designs too which was lovely and Robbie even said he could put something together on the computer for her. He's so good with graphics on that thing.

Sarah and I then cooked a roast dinner and there were a few times when we were alone that I thought to myself to tell her or at least say that I needed to talk to her about something important but I couldn't. Everytime I went to open my mouth about it, something stopped me, something in my heart just froze the words from escaping.

Everyone was so happy and it's been a few weeks since we all had this type of weather to be sitting outside to eat too. Even if it was a roast dinner.

Mum joined us for dessert as she had various clubs to attend today. She sat with Robbie to go over some book review thingy that he had to do for school the next day. He always leaves things until the day before, certainly doesn't get that from me. LOL.

It was just a really nice day today and time to relax before the start of chemo tomorrow. I must admit, I'm dreading it a bit. I guess it's just something I will have to get used to, for a good while yet it seems.

Please help me chemo - help me to stay around a bit longer than pops did.

*Note to self: Take ipod to chemo.

June 17th

Started my chemo sessions today.

What a joke of an ordeal that was!

My stupid veins wouldn't play ball. The ladies said that they think I had gotten too stressed so I must try and calm down before the next one. It was ok once it was all done and the nurses there were so nice about it.

There were around eight of us in the room but it was still eerily quiet. Strange feeling.

Everyone sat silent either reading or listening to their private music on earphones.

A few people had someone with them and although this made me feel a little sad to begin with, I knew that I just needed to be here alone., for now anyway.

I don't know how Karl or Sarah would cope if I asked them to sit there with me and why should they have to spend that time there?

It was boring for me and I wouldn't want to burden

them with it.

Maybe that's wrong of me though, maybe I should give them the benefit of the doubt and just blurt it to them, one of them...oh I don't know...I think it's best this way for the time being.

I have to learn to cope with it all myself first and then maybe, just maybe, they can be here. I'll have someone here soon...maybe... :(

It was over quite quickly really and I was glad to get some fresh air.

I've told Karl that I have extended my working hours to five oclock making the lame excuse that the kids are now old enough to walk home and be there until we get in.

All this just so that I can go and have the treatments without him wondering where I am.

I hate lying to him but I'm not ready to see his hurting eyes looking back at me! I feel like shouting at myself sometimes for betraying him like this.

He's so excited about his new contract at work and I don't want to take that away from him with my rubbish news.

How crazy am I being right now?

I've never lied to him, the whole time we've been together, all these years!

It'll be ok...I'll be fine, we WILL be ok, one day soon....

Goodnight diary.

xxJanexx

June 18th

So last night, I fell asleep in Karl's arms again. Chemo must've taken it out of me more than I thought.

He left one of his funny love notes on my pillow. If only he knew how much that meant to me.

Another memory to treasure I guess, but for how long?

I overslept but got to chemo with minutes to spare and even managed to squeeze in a visit with James and Pops.

James lent me a book, it was one of his mums so I must take care of it. I'm going to get through it while at the chemo. It seems like it has been ages since I held an actual physical book since getting my Kindle. I love the convenience of it but must admit, holding the book feels nice for a change.

Anyone else smell the pages? Or is it just me who is a bit of a weirdo.
LOL :) x

I had another catch up with Anna today about her wedding - she's one of the nurses there, really lovely girl and so excited about her big day coming soon.

She knew the book I was reading too, said she had read it and borrowed it from a lady who was in there for chemo.

I wondered if it could've been James' mother but no, I think that would be extra weird, well not weird but just too much coincidence, strangely.

I so remember all the planning for our wedding - I loved every minute of it. I must get the album out to look at the pictures again - it was such an amazing day.

*Note to self: Dig out the wedding album, take some pics to show Anna next time she's in.

There's been a few people missing for a week now. I know the reason deep down but don't want to admit to myself why they are no longer there. :(

Don't cry, don't cry!

Night Diary.xx

July 1st

I've missed so many days writing in here, I don't know where the time is going these days. It seems like all I do is work, then have the chemo sessions which are taking over my life and wading through the days and weeks way too fast.

Sarah rang today while I was in the clinic, another person I absolutely hate lying to. Told her I was in the blooming library, which she knows I do love going to, so that made it a little easier.

She has never lied to me, that I know of anyway, and she's my bestest friend in the whole world. We've told everything to each other through the years and now I'm keeping this massive secret from her.

What sort of friend am I? I'm sure I'll have to tell her at some point, she's very inquisitive at times and hiding stuff will soon become a no no. She's going to notice the signs that I am ill, I'm sure.

I'm looking forward to the weekend away with her, I just hope I can take my tablets without her seeing. She wouldn't be ready just yet for this news either so I can't slip up.

The clinic gave me a supply of pills ready to take away on the hen weekend. Can't believe how quickly that's come round but it will be great to see everyone.

*Note to self: get a disguise bottle for pills.

I met up with James for a bit, going to miss him over the few days I'm away. I had a mad idea that maybe I could set him up with Sarah??? :) He'd make a lovely husband for her - they are both such beautiful people and suit each other.

Maybe I'll chat to him about it first, he might not be ready to move on just yet.

He's beginning to feel like my little brother, someone I can take care of somehow - help him deal with his past as he's helping me cope with what's going on in my crazy life right now.

Who knows?? Maybe I can do this for him - for both of them.

Off to dream of ways to couple them up.

Goodnight dear diary.x

July 2nd

The weekend away will soon be here, only a few days to go and I must try and remember my stories.

CANNOT slip up and upset it.

I had a good chat with James today about it all.

I think he understands my reasons - I hope he does anyway...being the only person who knows, I don't have anyone to compare his thoughts to.

He spoke a bit more about his childhood, he has a brother but doesn't see him much at the moment.

Apparently he doesn't live too far away but they've just lost touch a bit since he split from his wife. He said they've spoken but he can't talk about his mum with him. Maybe it's just too painful for them both?.

Being an only child myself, I felt sad for him really.

I always dreamt of having a little sister or brother when I was younger. I know mum had problems after my birth and didn't want to risk being poorly again.

Anyway, James - I didn't want to push it as to the reasons why, he's quite a private person and I would hate to ruin the friendship we have.

He really is my saviour right now so I'll keep my thoughts to myself.

Bye for now.x

July 4th

HEN WEEKEND WITH GIRLS - YAY!

This afternoon, we go on the hen weekend and I really can't wait.

Just going to try and forget about all this horrible crappy c-word for a few days and enjoy some time away in Norfolk with the girls.

I will try and write in this while we are away but I need to be so careful with anyone seeing it, especially not Sarah seeing any of the content :(

See you in full on Sunday. x

We 've arrived and it's just soooo lovely here, it's a really cute place.
Think Sarah has already pulled - Carlos is his name and we think he's italian or spanish. I don't think she really cares but he is rather lush. He helps out here.

I think she's hoping he will do some topless gardening or butt naked butler service. LOL...

She's such a flirty one but we love her! Even flirting

on the way in the car, she's hilarious.

Scribbling some notes quickly while she's in the loo, then we are out for a meal just the two of us tonight.

Looking forward to it so much...xxx

July 5th

HEN WEEKEND :) - Dinner and dancing.

No time to write much here tonight - explain in full on Sunday. :(

I'm feeling sad and angry with myself and just want to chill out, not write more sadness tonight.

Sorry.xx

July 6th

I'm home and phew what a weekend that was!

Firstly, me and Karl are going out tonight so I'm scribbling away as quickly as I can while he's busy sorting food for Sarah and the kids.

The Hen weekend didn't quite go to plan basically. :(Not for the bride to be and the other girls but for Sarah and I.

It was really lovely to spend time with all the girls but, the dreaded happened - I told Sarah!

Not on the agenda for the weekend but I had no choice this time so...Sarah knows the truth, she knows I am ill and I'm not going to get better which I didn't want her to know for a long while, but, I should've known something was going on after the stop at the services.

My stupid clumsiness falling over when we stopped for coffee, meant she saw the pills that I forgot to disguise as vitamins they all tumbled out of my bag and I was too slow to grab them.

Jeez, why did I trip anyway? I'm getting more

clumsy by the week it seems and now I feel like I nearly ruined the weekend, for her especially.

God I hope she forgives me. I love her so much and now she's so sad. :(The sadness I didn't want to see, the sadness I've been trying to protect her from all these weeks now.

Deep down, I knew she had seen something suss with the pill bottle, but I hoped she wouldn't ask about them or that I could make her think they were something different.

Who was I kidding? She doesn't miss a trick that one. Bloody menopause pills, really??? Urghhh. As if she was going to believe that one!

When I finally fessed up, well, it was horrid, her face, her beautiful caring and loving face! :(

She was so upset, bless her and I should've known that she would be there for me no matter what, even with this sort of news!
I've made a promise to her now to keep her involved any way I can but she's also agreed to keep it to herself for now anyway. I know she'll keep to that for as long as I need her to.

In some way, I'm sort of glad I have her to talk to. It doesn't make the situation any better really though. I hate it so much and seeing her that sad was so heartbreaking for me. I don't think I've ever seen her face hurting as much as that since her parents died.

What else can we go through as friends, Jesus.
No more secrets please, surely, this has to be the ultimate secret.

Seeing Karl and the kids tonight when I got back made me forget the sadness for a little while. I have missed them so much and can't wait for our date night later on. It's been way too long and I'm promising myself now to go out there and enjoy my husband. Make it special for him...for us..x

We made love before the twins arrived back and it felt so magical - can you say sex feels magical? Well it did and I love him even more today than ever. I don't know why, I guess every moment like that will feel even more special from now on. :)xxx

Paula rang shortly afterwards - I must remember to ask them not to call me when I'm at home or certain times - I think Karl could see I was trying to hide the caller - maybe not, maybe I'm just extra paranoid that certain people will be suspicious of me or find out when I'm not ready for them to. Grr, deceit! :(

Mum dropped the kids off and teased me about having a date herself, she's a cheeky one, she really is but it would be nice to see her with someone to love again.

I promised pops I would try and find her someone to be with - I must, she deserves to be loved again.

*Note to self: Get mum a date this year :)

Signing off - Gotta get dressed to impress my man. :) x

July 7th

Our date night was awesome.

We went to a new Thai place in town and the food was sooooo yummy. :)

I was still tired from the busy and eventful weekend and in a bit of pain towards the end of the night too; running in the rain didn't help.

It was lovely being with him even though I kept getting tearful and blamed the fact that we were chatting about old times to cover up my heartbreak.

It felt more special than it has in a while. I know in my heart he is going to be so upset when I tell him the truth but I still can't manage to do it just yet. He's so happy with work and that, I don't want to ruin it for him.

It's wonderful to see him smiling and laughing. He seemed to glow even more tonight than usual and when he looks at me with those big puppy eyes, I just melt like ice cream in hot sun. I can't resist him sometimes.

Man, I love him soooo much. <3

He talked about making evenings out more of a regular thing, just us two, once a month. Sounds perfect for the 'normal' couple but I know it won't happen, well, not in the long term anyway. He doesn't obviously know it but I don't feel we are 'normal' by any means now and we won't have that long left to do it.

Jesus, why is this happening to me, to us...and why now when we have so much left to do together as a family.
:(

C-word - you really are breaking my heart as well as killing my body. Grrrr. I hate you!

Sarah was fast asleep when we got in so she stayed over. I know she had an early start so will have to catch up with her over the next few days.

Quick catch up with James this morning too.

Before work as well - I'm getting good at this rushing around business, although I was ten minutes late for work but hey, no-one noticed. No harm done.

Work was interesting but too tired to write about it tonight, fill you in tomorrow.

Night night. x

July 8th

This week is getting more complicated by the day it seems.

Update on the work thing: we had a meeting about the lack of clients that has been hanging over Carol's head for a few months so it was decided that the company had to let some people go to save some money.

For some reason, it became clear to me that I needed to tell her the truth and put myself forward to leave. I won't be able to work there in a few months anyway so I'd rather someone else's job was saved.

It was horrible.

She was so sad and the look in her eyes made me feel even worse. About everything, lying to her, telling her, making all this shit up day after day.

This is exactly why I can't tell Karl, Mum and certainly not the children. Oh my goodness, I can't think of it without wanting to burst into tears. It kills me inside, just the thought of telling them gets me emotional, what would I be like actually doing it? When is that likely to be - I have no idea! I don't want to know.

Anyway, I have come up with this crazy story that we have won a sum of money on a work lottery thing; (saw it on a newspaper in reception), who knows if it will work and Karl will believe me but I must try.

It's the only way I can cope with it at the moment, I can't just say I'm leaving work without a good reason. He would know Carol wouldn't make me redundant.

He will understand one day...I hope :(

*Note to self: Get my stupid story straight in my head!

July 9th

Work was weird today.

I started packing up my things ready to leave tomorrow. It's happened so quickly but it will mean I can get on with the other things I want, or need to do.

I want to write letters for everyone for when...well for when it's time, when it's over. :(

Trying to work out what I need to keep and what can stay there for the next person who is taking my office.

I will miss the place so much and my little office has been a haven for me over the past few years.

I've been so lucky and will always be grateful to Carol for helping me do this.

Florida will be our first call when I get this money through - it's somewhere we all have talked about going to, and now we can!

Thanks to my poxy lies anyway.

Thinking ahead already - I'm just hoping I can cope with it out there.

Apparently, the heat can be pretty intense during August.

*Note to self: DO NOT FORGET...fake cheque to show Karl tomorrow.

Night xx

July 10th

So, that is it! :/

No more working - it is going to be no more for me anyway. Carol knows the situation now and has given me a way out of some of the worrying.

I've just got to keep up this fake storytelling and try and just enjoy this time I have left with my crew at home, pretending that I am still going to work.

Perry was so sweet when I left, I'm hoping I will be around to see his baby when it arrives but honestly, I doubt it the way I've been feeling lately.

I'm going to tell Karl about the money later and hopefully my story will be convincing enough.

I popped by to speak to James about it all. As usual, he supported my choice to make this crazy story up to Karl and the kids.

He helped me store all my office bits for now so I didn't have to bring them home. What a palaver! Really?

What the heck am I doing?

LIES, LIES, LIES!!!

I hate you Cancer!!

I hate myself for all this deceit.

To the most important people in my life too.

WHY....???? :(

Urghhhh :(xx

July 11th

So there we go, I've done it - I've told the biggest lie to my husband, EVER!

Something I never thought I would do - lying to the most important person in my life, well one of them anyway.

God I hope this works out.

I think he seriously thought I was going to tell him that we were pregnant again, if only it was that. I've never wanted it to be something so different before. A new baby, a new life would be so much better than me losing my life, them losing their mother, wife, daughter.

That's the awful truth of what's going to happen now instead of something really exciting like a new baby.

Jeez!
This is so hard but I have to try and protect them for as long as I can. I have to, don't I?

Why am I even questioning this, if I revealed all this now, the holiday probably wouldn't happen.

Karl would never go away to Florida if he knew the truth. He'd make up some excuse that I needed to stay home, rest, take it easy, get second opinions...maybe, I don't know.

I'm feeling so confused.

His face though, when I told him my stupid made up nonsense lottery tale, he was so cute. Talking about going off to Miami and all the fun parks he wants to get booked in. :)

If only he knew, but no, he can't know. I want him to be happy, smiling like he was tonight.
I'm going to let him plan whatever he wants while we are away, this is his time to go for it and not have to worry like I am about everything.

We've decided to keep it from the kids until the day we go, they are going to be so surprised.

*Note to self: Book a dolphin swim experience for them.

I will make sure that this holiday is one for them to remember long after I'm gone.

Florida here we come! xxx

July 11th

I went to tell James the news today about the holiday and he's excited for us all.

I'm going to miss seeing him though. Hope he'll be ok while I'm away. I'm sure he will. He's been looking at some of my work books but finds them quite boring. He's funny. He's also amazing at flower displays and I kind of leave the laying of flowers to him now because he does it better than me.

When we first met, I did wonder about him, why he'd befriended me like he did.

I'm not usually suspicious of people but it did cross my mind - I mean, a total stranger becoming almost like another best friend in a matter of weeks.

But no, he's just too lovely to be anything sinister so I will carry on seeing him and dream of getting him together with Sarah soon.

I want to get him a gift from Florida but how would I explain that to Karl - he has no idea about James and our meetings. It's something I'm keeping between the two of us because for me, it's an escape from normality at times. He doesn't want to talk about cancer and dying, he's just there to chat like friends do and it feels nice to have that, to have this sort of relationship with him.

Is that wrong? Am I wrong for keeping him to myself? Do I deserve to have such a friend and keep him secret? Maybe he would like to meet my family, maybe it is time he met Sarah?

Questions, questions...I'm always asking myself questions.

Is it because I know I'm wrong in hiding this stuff, is it because I know I'm doing the right thing by trying to protect my family from this bloody thing that's killing me softly and silently?

Urghhhh, if only I had all the answers. :/

If only this wasn't bloody happening at all!

Night...xxx

July 13th

We booked the flights and a handful of trips for Florida today, we also booked Sarah's ticket to come join us for the 2nd week and it's going to be great seeing her face when we show her.

I'm so glad Karl didn't mind her coming along. He loves her like a sister and knows how much we mean to each other.

It will mean we can do some shopping together there too. Can't wait for that! She's going to be so shocked when I tell her she's coming! yay!

Not long to go and all can be revealed and the kids.

July 14th

My entries in here seem to be getting shorter and I keep missing days out completely.
Sorry diary. xx

Chemotherapy and learning how to pretend to go to work are taking up so much time and thinking, I almost keep forgetting to keep track of things in here.

Karl is blissfully unaware of the fact that I get dressed to go to work as normal, see the kids off to school, as normal and then 'go to work' as normal!

Except I don't do anything 'normal' anymore.

I visit James or do some housework or read or go to my bloody chemo appointments, see the doctor, see the nurse, cry with pops, make plans for when the time comes... :(
Urghh, it's taking over my life.

My life is full of lies right now. How long will I be able to keep this craziness up? It's insane but I'm finding it easy to come up with stuff quicker if needed, when needed.

Robbie called my mobile and I had the radio on at home, he even asked me why the music was on at work. I came up with the scenario that we had some musician clients in.

I mean what the hell..??!!

At least it was a station he wouldn't know the artists of, thank goodness for old school radio stations. (Loved the 80's). :)

I'm thinking of how my hair may look while I'm away and have ordered a few hats to try on. It will help to keep the sun off my face too but I've never been one for hats so god knows how it will look. Hey ho! Got to try these things hey.

I know my hair is getting thinner, I just know how it feels and what I see in the bottom of the shower tray when I wash it.

I've taken to gathering it all up in tissue and flushing it down the loo, just so Karl doesn't notice it in the en-suite bin. Not that he empties that often, bless him but just in case. If needed, I'll just tell him it's that time of year - you know when we shed our hair, like dogs do!!!

All these things I have to now think of on a daily basis, just to pretend and lie! :(

Oh I'm rambling on again about nothing particularly interesting. lol.

Goodnight. x

July 15th

Today's chemo was rough. I don't know why and I'm soooo tired this evening.

I bought another mobile today so that the clinic can call me or text me on that instead of my main phone.

I don't know if this is the way to go but I think Karl has been noticing me trying to hide my other phone a bit more.

I might just be paranoid about it but if it helps keep my sordid secret for a while longer then so be it.

Signing off now, I need some sleep.

Zzzzz
xxJxx

July 16th

I've started writing letters to everyone for after - after I'm gone :(

I'm going to ask Sarah if she can give them out once...once I've gone. :(

I mean I'll ask her beforehand, when the time is right.

Not making sense again am I?

Anyway, I want everyone to know individually what they meant to me and give them a few of my memories between us and I want to include a few of my favourite photos in each envelope.

It's so hard though, trying to get so many years of feelings down on paper without it turning into some school essay size thing.

I feel like I'm writing a book to Karl especially. We've been through so much together and it's annoying that we won't have those old age memories now.

No growing old and grey together, no seeing the

children's children, weddings, special birthdays and that. Like we planned as new lovers back in the day.

Grrrr....I get so angry inside about it all - the whole situation stinks.

Mrs Nice, that's what they call me!

I may be Mrs Nice most of the time, (that's what everyone seems to think anyway), but this thing that's taking its toll on me, taking me away from my beautiful family and friends is making me hate, making me angry every day that ticks by.

Every day that I realise is ticking by too quickly and one less day I will have with these guys. This family that I adore with all my heart and all my soul.

Everything I do is for them.

All I wanted out of life was to be happy, settle down with the love of my life, and watch the children grow up, grow old, grey and wrinkly with Karl; see mum fall in love all over again, see my best friend settle down with someone, finally at some point, bless her.

She must find someone before I go, she's too gorgeous to be alone forever.

Maybe I could help her, change her mind of being single forever.

Maybe, before it's too late for me to help??

I'm soooo tired now....

Night night for now. :(

July 18th

The kids had a little spat today. I hate to see them arguing as they're so close most of the time.

I'm not really sure what it was about and they both didn't seem to want to chat about it.

There were a lot of slamming doors and stomping around.

Hormones I guess - I remember being a teenager and flipping at the drop of a hat!

Hopefully they'll make up by tomorrow.

It's been a funny few days and I'm feeling as though I'm not writing as much as I should, sorry diary. :(

July 25th

It's been exactly a week since I wrote here.

Things have been mad since revealing the money story and booking all the exciting holiday plans with Karl.

The days and weeks are going way too fast for my liking but Florida is nearly here now.

My new notebook is filling up nicely with letters for everyone.

I'm going to try and find a special box to keep them in and store them at the shed with James. Maybe I could look in the charity shops in town this week before we get off.

Sarah can get it when needed.

*Note to self: Get coloured envelopes, look for a tin.

August 9th

FLORIDA, FLORIDA, FLORIDA!

Today is the day...we are going to Florida!

It's come round so quickly and we have so much planned.

It's going to be soooooo good and I'm so excited :)

The kids came home from their friends' and Karl announced it to them. He even set up the Go-pro thing, to record their reactions, that's something we will be able to watch again and again.

I will never tire of seeing their beautiful faces staring back at us like they did today.

It was just so adorable, and something I will treasure for however many months I can. Warmed my heart, it really did.

I must try and remember to take this diary with me.

Note to self: pack Diary in my handbag to keep it from any eyes getting to it. :/

I went to see James quickly to say goodbye and made it back home just in time. I couldn't help it, I love to chat with him but then I had to go to the shop because again, I had lied to Karl to say I had to get some toiletries and bits.

Maybe after the holiday I could get James to come and meet everyone finally - they'd all love him too. Robbie would find him cool I expect. Lol...

Right, best get off now, Karl has just called upstairs that we need to go.

Florida, here we come! :) xxx YAY....xxx

August 24th

Yep, that's right, I forgot to take this blooming thing to Florida - what a surprise! :/

Damn, I hope I can remember everything we got up to.

My mind is so preoccupied with everything right now including all the stupid stories and lies I have to keep making up.

I could've sworn I put this in my bag on the day we left but no, it was sitting on my bedside cabinet!

Good job I went upstairs first when we arrived home.

Anyway, here goes some catching up. Fingers crossed I've got it all safely stored in my head.

<u>Florida:</u> Just one word for this place - AMAZING. Sun, fun and laughter - what more could we have wanted.

<u>Karl:</u> I think I can safely say that he has enjoyed this holiday somewhat. I've never seen him smiling and laughing so much for so many days in a

row. To watch him and the kids has been truly amazing and I've loved every moment of it.

Such special memories have now been implanted into my mind and it makes me smile through any pain that decides to try and dampen my heart and into my entire soul.

I will not let this beat away those times that I can remember now for any time that I may have left with them.

<3 He's my true love - he really is the only one I could have ever loved and I'm going to miss him...well, I suppose I can't miss him if I'm no longer here.

Oh damn it...tears just crept out. :(

<u>The Twins</u>: I don't think I've ever seen them so happy either and so full of joy and excitement every single morning. I know they have had friends who've been to Florida and always wanted to go so this meant the world to me. To be able to get them there, even if I've lied to them - to all of them really, apart from Sarah who does actually know the truth.

I could see it in their eyes when Sarah and I went off for a few hours - they seemed sad to not be able to spend every minute with me, with us. Especially Cassie as we said we were shopping and I think deep down she wanted to come along but obviously, we weren't shopping the whole time. I had to rest at some points during the stay out there - it was exhausting so Sarah helped cover up saying we were having a spa day etc. I can't thank her enough for being there for me and going along with my bloody lies too. I shouldn't ask her to do that, especially as she loves the kids soooo much.

They know how important Sarah is to me though, so I'm just hoping they understood, even if we weren't completely truthful with them.

Seeing them meeting new friends, playing carefree and worry free was all my heart wanted for this break and I'm sort of sad it's over now.

I know the day may come when I have to sit them both down and talk to them about what's going on with me but I'm hoping it's not that soon. I want the memories and the joy of the holiday to stay with us for a while longer.

Please damned c-word - don't take my body over too soon, let me have these happy times for a little bit longer, please, for my kids, my Karl and my mum. I don't want to leave them just yet, please.???

Sarah: Well, she was blown away with her ticket invite to join us in the second week. I gave it to her at the airport, she came to see us off. That was pretty cool to be able to do, thank goodness for this money story.
It was so nice to have her there especially when I needed to slip away for treatment or take my tab-

lets in secret away from Karl and the kids. She had my back as per usual.

<u>Mum</u>: she hadn't wanted to come on this, her passport had run out last year and she told me she didn't want to travel that far anymore. I would've loved to have her with us but I understand her reasons so we got her a few nice pressies anyway.

<u>FUN, FUN, FUN</u>: The many parks and excursions were soooo tiring though but I could easily blame the holiday as to why I was so bad. I think everyone was knackered by the end of each day so…no-one thought any different as to why it seemed to take it out of me more than usual. I think I managed to keep the stupid lies going for the two weeks we were there.

<u>Dolphins</u>: I booked the kids and Karl a swimming with dolphins experience and scuba diving while I went to the chemo clinic out there. They got some beautiful photos of the day while I snuck out to see a doctor there. Thank goodness for this money allowing me to get some advice and treatment out there.

Pretending I was having another spa day because I didn't like swimming - what a nightmare, I could've sat on the side watching or just paddled in the shallow end but, no…lies, lies, lies.

If they knew what I'd really been up to…

I don't know if they'd forgive me for not telling

them - I don't know if they WILL forgive me if they find out after but...I had to do it alone.

It's for the best though isn't it?

Questioning myself yet again. ????? :/

*Note to self: stop being so hard on myself - I'm trying to do what's best. :(

<u>Helicopters!!</u> : Karl came up with a crazy idea of us having a helicopter trip and I just went with it - I mean why not! I'm certainly not going to get the chance to do that again am I! The kids were totally in awe of it, we've never known them so quiet.

<u>New friends:</u> In the second week, we met Brad, Marie and their children, Daniel & Sophie.

Their beautiful children are around the same ages as the twins so it was lovely for Cass and Rob to have them to mess around with for a few days.

I was so shocked to learn that Marie has terminal skin Cancer. She looked so weak at times and has to be in a wheelchair constantly now. She can't walk too much because she gets tired out and has medication going into her all the time.
She's such a lovely person, and so brave with it all, they are such a lovely family, her and Brad make a gorgeous couple and Karl got on great with him.

So sad for them though as they all know it's not long until they have to say goodbye to their mum, wife. :(

I couldn't believe how brave the children were being though, knowing that this would be their last holiday together with their mum. I think meeting them has been great for all of us and maybe it might help our kids when the time comes.

Mine don't even know that this has been our last one.

The children have swapped addresses and social media accounts so that they can keep in touch, it was so nice to see them enjoying themselves doing what children do! :)

*Note to self: Facetime them next week to see how Marie is doing.

The thought of my children knowing my secret hurts me so much and to be honest, I don't think we would've had such a great time over there if they'd known the truth.

Karl would just have worried constantly that I was doing too much or getting too tired and I know the kids would've felt guilty for leaving me on the days they had trips and adventures.

God I wish I was going to see them grow up and have their own children.

It's just not going to be, is it, surely not? This thing

is a battle that I feel I'm beginning to lose and it makes me more angry by the day but more sad that I can't be in their futures...our future as a family.

There was a tough moment on the plane as we headed home when Karl mentioned not being able to visit Miami like he wanted us to. He said he'd take me next year for our wedding anniversary - I just smiled and nodded back at him. He was still too excited to notice that I didn't really agree.

Deep down, I know that won't happen because I won't be here.

It will be over for me by then and that breaks my heart so much.

The fact that I won't see another anniversary with him, the fact that he will be alone on that special day when usually we would sit down, watch the wedding video, look at the photos or have a romantic night out somewhere that had memories for us.

I'm trying to write through tears once again as I think about not being here with this lot.

Why? Why? You stupid cancer. :(

Why do you have to exist!?
If it wasn't for this pretend lottery money, all of this would not have happened this year, I'm sure of it.

We may have gone somewhere on holiday but this

had to be the ultimate destination - for my final holiday with the gang!

I'm so excited to get to see James soon, it seems like ages since we spoke. Hope he's been ok.

Once the kids are back at school and Karl is at work, normal chatting and meetings can resume.

It's just been so hard to slope off with them all here and honestly, I want to be with them as much as I can. James will understand, I just know.

As much as I want to see him, he'll be the friend he is and know it's for the best…

See you soon J.Cooper.x

So that was basically the lowdown of the holiday - there's probably days more memories I could write about but this entry is getting way too long!

My chemo starts back in a few days. I don't know if it's worth having anymore if I'm honest but I guess even if it gets me a few more weeks on this planet, with the people I adore, then it's worth it.

My super not Normal life will resume soon.

Signing off to get all the washing done now, speak soon. X

September 4th

I've laid off the diary for a bit so sorry about that...

Felt the need to just concentrate on being with my little family at nights instead of writing.

School has started, another year up for the twins.

Only seems like yesterday they had started there. This is such an important year for them too with exam prep so I must try and spend some time with them going over what subjects they'd like to take.

James has been fine - I should've known he'd be alright.

I mean it's not like I'm holding him together is it? He's the one who is there for me every time, keeping me strong and happy.
He has had the full low down of the holiday - I had so much to tell him about. Hope I didn't bore him too much. :/

I don't know what I'd do without him right now, he arrived at the most awkward moment but has been an absolute godsend to me, never moaning or getting sad with me, just happy times and all the craziness that he has had to deal with too.

He opened up a bit more about his wife leaving him today. I cannot imagine what the hell he thought when that happened. Such a shame for him but he sees the funny side of it and does make me laugh.

I don't laugh often enough anymore, not when I'm alone anyway.

My fake smiles and laughter sometimes is hard work - I don't want anyone to suspect that I'm in pain or feeling so heartbroken by this disease that's taking me somewhere I'm really not ready to go to!

Just a few more months, please - keep me going to Christmas - I want to see that tree one more time, just one more year.

Please...xxx

September 8th

Where are the days going???

I have missed so many days writing again!

How am I too busy to write in here when I'm not working anymore. I must try harder so I can get these days written.

Does it matter..??

I don't know, maybe, maybe not but in some way, I think it helps me come to terms with the lies and deceit I'm throwing out each day to my beautiful family.

Chatted to Sarah earlier as we grabbed a coffee on her lunch break - she thinks I should tell mum and Karl soon.

Not in agreement on that one just yet.

My head says yes go ahead, tell them all, let them in, let them help but, NO, my heart says...No, no...it says I don't want their sad faces looking back at me, it says my heart is breaking enough right now with only Sarah and James to talk to about it.

So, for now, I must keep the lies going - I must. :(
xx

September 11th

Today has been horrid and I feel horrid.

Cassie has been having some trouble at school so the school rang us but only managed to get through to Karl, I missed the calls, texts and more importantly, the meeting.

Why did I miss it all?

Because of you - stupid, horrible, wretched Cancer!

You have made me miss this and I hate you again and again.

I HATE YOU!

I was having chemo to try and stop you taking over but you won again. Grrrrr. :(

Cancer 1000 - Me a big fat ZERO ...that's how it seems anyway. You are winning big time.

I feel like such a bad mother tonight and can't even explain where I've been to Karl or Cass.

Karl dealt with it and told me not to worry about the fact I wasn't there. but how can I, I'm her bloody mother and I should've been there.

I feel like I'm getting too caught up in this bloody illness and my mind isn't working normally.

Maybe I can chat to the doctor about reducing the meds or maybe they could give me something a little stronger to help with the tiredness and confusion at times. More questions about it all to myself!

Cassie hasn't told us exactly what they've been saying, just some girls being nasty, but I guess she will open up when she's ready.

Bloody teenage girls! They can be so cruel sometimes.

I told Karl some stupid lie about a client that I had to go and see because she was scared of heights and couldn't come into my office to see me!!!

What a bloody joke!

But, he took it so, must have been convincing.

I'm not even at work for christ's sake.... :(

I keep saying bloody. I'm not usually a swearer but at the minute, I'm too angry. Sorry diary..x

I'm writing this while trying to relax in the bath, I needed to get it down here how I'm feeling and this is the only 'alone' time I've had today really.

I locked the door tonight so I could just be by myself.

Karl sounded a bit confused when he came upstairs to come and sit with me but I just couldn't face him. I feel like I may have blurted it all out to him tonight, that's how bad I've been feeling.

The bruises on my arms are getting worse, my weight is going down by the day and my hair...my nails - everything is getting taken over - I hope Karl doesn't start to notice me getting so horrible.

I want to stay beautiful to him, even if I don't like looking at myself anymore.

He will still love me I'm sure.

J xx

September 12th

By the time I finished in the bath last night, Karl was fast asleep and I couldn't budge him so I slept in the study.

This gave me some more time to think over the memories we have had over the years. I couldn't get to sleep for ages and I went over and over the thoughts of when he came to work and whisked me off my feet for my birthday.

Seeing my favourite musical in such an amazing way, he really did pull that one off brilliantly.

I loved him even more that night.

I didn't think I could love him anymore than I already did but he took my breath away with what he planned that evening. And in such a stylish way too, I felt absolutely beautiful.

Anyway, must get to sleep now, busy few days ahead. Xx

Night.xx

September 16th

<u>Meeting anniversary!</u>

Today is one of our special days. :))

All those years ago in college when Karl and I met for the first time.
Wow, that's flown by seriously fast - where have those 23 years gone? And boy have we fit a lot in.

Anyway, I'm writing here this morning so I don't miss a day again. Hoping Karl and I will be too busy tonight for me to worry about writing my diary! Hee hee…

Speak later. X

Update: I went into town after chemo and bought a new little sexy number to show Karl later. I hope he likes it. ;)

A nice little red number this time. Cheeky!
Also bought a few head scarves online to try out - no idea how I'm going to cope wearing them - tried quickly this morning but not any good at them as yet. Will have to get Sarah to help me.

The kids are going on sleepovers so we have the whole house to ourselves.

I'm thinking about getting him to order an indian, not really up for going out for dinner and it will make the evening last longer if we stay in. I'm so excited for tonight.

Saw James today too - he had some new gorgeous flowers to lay on the graves. Such a gent but I must try and remember to get them next week. He's always bringing them before I get the chance.

Speak soon diary!

I have to get myself looking beautiful for my man. xxx

September 18th

It's been a few days since writing in here, just been so sad and upset at what happened the other night.

Our 'anniversary' night didn't go as planned, not by a long shot.

Karl went to my 'work' and guess what, he found out that I no longer work there.

Well for a start that's what he found out! Then it got even worse!

Carol tried to call me but stupidly, I hadn't charged my phone, hadn't even bothered to look at it during the day.

I was too excited and thinking about the great anniversary night we were about to have that I just didn't bother - what a huge mistake that has turned out to be!

He now knows the whole truth - all of it and I'm completely heartbroken but even more than that, Karl is crushed to pieces with my news.

We had a huge argument and it was awful - just so

awful. :(

I've never seen him react that. He was so angry and then so hurt. I've never wanted to hurt him like this and I am so angry at myself now for not just telling him in the first place.

Why did I do this to him?

What a pathetic wife I've been to him over these past few months! How could I have thought he would react any different though - lying - something we always said we wouldn't do.
At first, he thought I was having an affair - jeez, I wish I was instead of this friggin nonsense.

It would make things a whole lot easier to take maybe.

Oh I don't know, am I now being even more stupid?

He stormed out and I didn't know what else to do but call Sarah who was here in a flash helping me sort my face out, sort out my mashed brain and just be there.

What a gem she is! I don't know what I'd do if I didn't have that girl in my life. Putting her through this as well, it's horrid of me.

She was so upset when we were trying to sort out my hair - she was brushing it for me, trying to get it looking nice and a big clump came out and it really shocked her. She's not seen that happen yet

and I felt really bad for her. The sadness I could see in her eyes - just heartbreaking.
Mum dropped the twins back the next day, she said that I looked a bit peaky but I had to of course, assure her I was fine.

Lies lies...urghhh.

I hugged her a little bit tighter than usual - I hope she doesn't suspect anything. She looked as though she knew I was hiding something.

We made love last night and it was so beautiful. It felt like...I don't know, different, special, more special than other times...???

Does that sound weird? :/

I just wish I could have frozen the moment for a while longer, he makes me feel like the most beautiful woman on earth even if I've hurt him with my bloody lies.

We've been through so much as a couple - I wouldn't be the person I am today if he hadn't been there for me so much. He's my soulmate and I hate the thought of leaving him let alone hurting him the way I just have.

If ever you find this Karl, please know that I love you so much and I'm so so sorry I hurt you like this..xx

Anyway, I may take a break from this diary for

another few days to try and get my head together with Karl on where to go next.

Bye,
Jane.x

September 20th

Sarah and I went to London today, it was such a laugh. I actually had so much fun, a lot more than I thought I would.

And after this week's events with Karl, it was a much needed session of laughter.

I needed to get some sort of hair piece, wig thing to help disguise my thinning hair so when I told her, she couldn't wait to get in touch with one of her drag queen friends, Danny.

So now, I have this natural looking wig to wear.

It's amazing what can be done with hair these days and surprisingly, it looks ok.

I didn't want anything too drastic like the ones Sarah was picking out!

She's hilarious. :)

This piece looks good for now.

My hair is getting thinner and weaker by the day and I don't want the kids to see it falling out or if I get any more bald patches, I'm sure Cass will notice. She loves my hair and always used to twiddle it in her fingers when she was having her bottle as a baby.

Anyway, we had a nice lunch and then we went to a little boutique near the station to find her a new dress. She looked ultra sexy in the one we chose and it got me thinking it was about time that I should mention James, so I did! :)

I was slightly nervous to reveal that I had a secret friend but I wanted them to meet and thought I may be the only one who could sort it out. Then it will be like my two best friends will be together.

She really needs to be with James and I'm determined to make it happen. She would never get round to meeting her soulmate if not, she's too much of a free spirit as she says.

She's agreed to meet him and give it a try anyway so I can't wait to see him later and tell him all about her now.

Exciting times!.x

September 21st

I forgot to speak to James yesterday about meeting with Sarah.

*Note to self: DO NOT forget J&S matchmaking.

Too busy showing off my poxy wig at first but then he really opened up about his mother, how she taught him to arrange flowers and her choice of treatments and the plans that she put in place.

It was lovely to hear him talking about her for a change.

Beats my boring cancer stress stories and trials at the moment.

We also chatted about hospices, turns out he wants to work in one at some point. I could see that as he's so caring and would be an asset to any patient and any hospice. Maybe I could grab a leaflet for him when I visit it.

I took my notebook and some new envelopes with me too so I could sit and write while I watched James sorting the weeds and flowers. He loves the idea and that means a lot. I was worried it may be too much for everyone but feel happier now that I'll have them all ready in time.

I've been reading him a few of my memories that I've been writing out in the letter. He just sits and listens to me go on sometimes but I love it and I love the time we have chatting.

I'm hoping to get all the photos printed out so I can add them into the letters. A nice family one in Florida would be great to print for all of them to have a copy.

Tired again now so popping off for a nap. Xx

September 22nd

Me and Karl went to the solicitors today to make sure my will was in order before I can't travel there or think about it clearly.

Not a nice thing to think about but I guess it's for the best.

I really hate all this planning my death and I wish I had more to give to the children. I know Karl will make sure they are supported and have anything they need in life once I'm gone.

I seem to be able to say that a bit more now, like it's finally sinking in that I will be gone soon.

Afterwards, I had a bit of a meltdown. Felt pretty foolish about it and felt bad for Karl, again! He really doesn't need me to do that to him. He has enough to deal with for goodness sake!

We also visited the hospice that Paula mentioned. He wanted to come and visit it with me and told me that he had told Adam, his boss, about every-thing. I don't know why that shocked me but it did. I just imagined he wouldn't tell anyone like I hadn't. I suppose it's nice that he has someone to tell, someone to talk to about it other than me I guess.

The hospice was lovely and the staff there are doing an amazing job dealing with what they have to do each day, each week - what superstars. **

At first, I wasn't sure about going in but we did and I'm sort of glad we did now.

Karl met a guy whose sister was in there. He's going to meet up with him I think. It's really nice for him to have a man to chat to I guess and apparently, he's been through the mill a few times already.

Poor thing.

Another win for Cancer it seems! :(

Mum's coming for dinner tonight, I've missed her so much these past few weeks.

Time for a nap now...x

September 23rd

SO....Mum came over last night and she knew something was up with me so...I told her.

Sarah was round too cooking dinner as Karl had gone out to meet Dave from the hospice.

I'd fallen asleep pretty quickly when we had gotten home - exhausting day so he hadn't wanted to wake me just to say he was going out. Love him.

Mum is so precious, she thought I was going to say that the reason I've been looking tired was because I was pregnant again - bless her...

If only! If only it was a new baby to bring joy to our family instead of this!

She was so upset but understood my reasoning. I know she will help out and support me with this. She's never been anything less than supportive of everything I've ever done.

My heart breaks for her having to deal with losing another family member to this thing and I'm so sad for her.

She told me that the kids have been asking questions about me and asking if I'm poorly.

I guess I've underestimated them too. They are such clever kids and the day will be here soon when I have to tell them too!

Urghhhh!!

DAMN IT....

Night...xxx

September 24th

Finally, I spoke to James today about meeting Sarah but he didn't quite take it the way I thought he would.

At first he wasn't really up for it and said something about it being time to leave me.??? Strange!

He says he doesn't want to come to the cemetery anymore, I guess he's ready to move on a bit more now but I've convinced him to meet her so now I need to make it happen for both of them. Yay, exciting...

I'd love to see them together before, well before I go.

He's moved the bench nearer to the graves so I can sit and watch him doing the weeding and such.

It's getting so hard to just kneel down or try and crouch down to lay the flowers so he's taking charge of all of that. So caring and thoughtful as he is. Just the perfect person for Sarah to have in her life! :)

I got really tearful at the thought of not seeing him

anymore and I just can't imagine him not being around, not having our funny chats.

I'll convince him otherwise, I'm sure I can. ;)

Robbie asked me if I was dying tonight. I had to lie to my little boy. His friend's mum wears a head-scarf because her hair has fallen out due to cancer so he put two and two together. But, what did I do...gave him five...lied again!!

Hopefully he believed me but I just feel terrible every time lies come out of my mouth. It's just so often.

Had a chat with Sarah regarding meeting James and she's up for it but will have to be at the week-end as she's on a course for work stuff. I can't wait! Yay :)

J x

September 26th

My days seem to be flying by even more quickly and I don't seem to have the energy at night to pick this thing up just to write a little bit sometimes.

Sorry, not much happening to write about. ;/

J.x

September 27th

Finally it's matchmaking day - I'm so excited for them.

Back later with some romance news. :))))) Hopefully!

WOOOHOOOO...!!

Excited ME!!

J

September 30th

Well…that was that! :(

I've missed writing for a few days because, well, the matchmaking thing for James and Sarah has not worked out at all! It did NOT work out!!

My brain has been completely smashed to pieces since Saturday and I'm so confused, sad and…feeling even more stupid than ever!

When we got to the cemetery, the second time, there was another guy there sitting on our bench and once we got talking, he explained who he was!

James' brother! I thought he looked familiar but what the hell…?

I can't quite believe what I'm about to write here but, it turns out that James…he…he had died a few years ago.
The guy sitting on our bench was Tom, James' older brother! The one we only chatted about recently saying he didn't see him that often and now…there he was!

He had come to visit James' grave on what would

have been his birthday.

His 40th birthday at that!

I can't get my head round it, hence the late entry and no further excitement regarding the Sarah/James match up mission that was a complete failure. :(

I'm in complete shock.

I have so many questions but no-one to ask, only myself and that doesn't even get me the answers I need right now.

Why didn't he tell me the truth?
Why did I have to find out like that?
Was he some sort of angel/spirit, sent to help me?
Was he just a figment of my imagination?
I really don't understand what's happened here though. I mean, I spoke to him, we chatted, he helped me cope at the most horrible time of my life and all the time...he wasn't even there really - he wasn't even alive!!! WHAT??!!

He lied to me so my guilt of fibbing to everyone is okay?

It's not just me who has been lying to people for months on end! James lied too or did he just not want to tell me the full truth of what happened to him let alone telling me that he was some sort of ghost sent to help me...Jesus...how mad does that sound in my head!

He killed himself after his wife left him. I knew about his wife leaving, I knew that she left him to be with another woman but what he hadn't told me was that she had been pregnant and he just couldn't cope with losing her and the baby.

He was going to be a father and she took that away from him - telling him she had lost the baby...why? Why? Why would you do that to someone? Someone so lovely as James - my friend James. My secret friend.

God knows what Sarah must think of me, she's promised not to mention it to Karl - he'll think I've lost the plot or something. I think she may do as well. She looked at me very strangely afterwards.

Maybe it's all the drugs I've been on - but he was there, he was...

Now what?! ?????

Xx confused xx

October 1st

Been thinking all day today - thinking hard.

About James - the man that wasn't there but was.

That just sounds too much, too mad - unreal, sur-real...

I'm still trying to get over the fact that he has never 'really' been here...or there - so confusing.

My mind has been racing as to what has gone on and how my brain has been playing these tricks on me.

I've not been one to believe in ghosts before but it's the only logic I have for this situation. He was a ghost spirit - sent to help me? Sent to confuse me?

Can't find any more words to write, too confused and so, so, sad :(

Goodnight.x

October 4th

Over the past week, I've come to my final conclusion about the events of last weekend.

So here goes...my brain's explanation - or my brain's explosion more like.

James - I really do feel as though he was sent to help me through this challenging time in my life, by who...I don't know,maybe pops, maybe just someone looking down on me knowing I needed that support, that all important special friend who had nothing to do with my family - an outsider to confide in.

The more I've thought about everything though, the more I see becoming clearer in my mind.

He wore the same clothes, he was always there no matter what time I would turn up, we never talked about phone numbers, where he lived, the normal everyday conversations that just didn't happen for some reason - why?

And the neck scarf that he always wore, the scarf that I just thought was a fashion thing for him, I now realise the importance of it and why he never changed it or went without wearing it - to hide the hanging marks from the way he died - his suicide…:(

Oh my goodness, I cannot help but cry for this man, for this circumstance…what's happened, what happened to him in his short life.

How tortured he must have felt and to then just put up with me whimpering and moaning when all the time I was still alive and he wasn't? I still had my life and he didn't. Now that sounds crazy.

His brother was so lovely - I hope he's ok - maybe I should've got his phone number so I could find out more about James and their past together. I'd love to find out more about him, instead of the tragedy that I now know. :(

James Michael Cooper - whoever you were, wherever you are now - thank you - Thank you so much.

Goodnight James - you were so special to me. Xxx

October 6th

Sarah has been truly amazing these past few days after our eventful non meeting etc and today, there she was again. Helping me cope with more heartache from this blasted thing that's taken over my life.

Another day, another round of sadness!

That's all life seems to consist of for me right now. For us as a family really.

The kids came home early with Sarah after Cassie had phoned her from school.

My phone was on silent while I had some chemo and I forgot to turn the volume back on when I got home for my meeting with Paula.

Some kids at school have been teasing them about my stupid headscarf and the bloody walking stick that I have to use these days so we had to sit down with them - I had to tell them the awful truth - had to reveal all to them this time and it was just as terrible as I thought it would be.

Their little faces killed me inside. I tried so hard to

keep the tears from coming out of my eyes.

I have tried to be strong for them for so long, trying to protect them from this anguish I've been feeling but they took it in and at first, I didn't know if they truly understood.

They did though, they do understand...and I feel sort of relieved in a way although I would've preferred to do it when I was more prepared.

They have been so brave tonight and I'm so proud of them both for coping with it so well.

Robbie asked if it was like Marie in Florida - stupidly I thought that he hadn't really taken much notice, being kids, I hoped they wouldn't have talked about it but it turns out they did a lot...
- I've underestimated my own children and their strength.

Failed mum status again. :(

I cannot imagine not being here and seeing them grow up but it's now reality isn't it, it's just not going to happen and I hate everything about that so much right now.

I hate you Cancer, I really really hate you soooo much!

What this thing is doing to me and more importantly to my family and beautiful best friend, is bloody horrible.

It is so unfair beyond reason. :(- I HATE IT...
xx

October 12th

We went to town today - just for some time out from home stuff really.

It was lovely to see all the Christmas displays already up in the shops, but I didn't enjoy it as much as I used to, before this dreaded c-word came into my life!

Karl spent most of the day pushing me around in a poxy wheelchair because I just don't have the energy to walk around for too long so he's hired one for the next few months. I felt like Marie - although she didn't moan like I am now.

Why do I always beat myself up about it all - it's not my fault...or is it?? If I had not been so busy or gone to the doctors when I first got worried about the lump, this could've been avoided - I may have been able to catch it in time before it spread???

I'm always questioning that very thing and it doesn't make it easier to digest in my brain. It doesn't make it easier to mend my broken heart - to mend the broken hearts of my family and friends. : (

I cry regularly nowadays, but most of the time, I try to hide away to do so - I don't want to upset the children, they've got enough to deal with knowing they won't have a mum soon.

I've heard Karl crying a few times - he doesn't know that and I won't tell him. That really breaks my heart, to think how sad he feels.

I don't want to die. :(

November 8th

I've been unable to write for a few weeks now.

Everyone knows about how poorly I am now and it sucks, it really sucks big time.

Things are really getting me down and I'm more tired than ever.

My hair is holding on but a few strands and I can't even have mirrors near me.

Even my eyebrows and lashes are nearly gone and I think I weigh about six stone - I'm so...ugly..:(

I don't want to be remembered like this.

:(

November 9th

Brad phoned this evening to say that Marie had gotten worse and they didn't expect her to see the month out. :(

It hit us all really hard but I think the kids were hit the hardest if I'm honest. They sent texts to Brad's kids after we told them.

God, I hope they are all coping okay...and I hope she's not suffering too much now.

I'm too sad to write much more tonight so I'm going to sign off now.

xxJ

November 14th

I felt a bit more perky today so the four of us went to London Zoo for the day.

It was lovely but I hated having to be confined to the wheelchair once again! There was no other way I would have got round it though. So many animals to see.

If only I could've run around with the kids like we used to. Playing cheeky monkeys like we did on their fifth birthday at Colchester Zoo.

Such good memories from that day. :)

The twins are probably getting a little bit old for the zoo now but actually, they seemed to enjoy it. I think they just liked being out of the house with me and Karl and somewhere a little bit different to cinema or bowling.

Cassie loved the elephants and giraffes whereas Robbie preferred the insects and creepy crawlies. He took some great photos with his new phone though. Impressive camera that is.

Although I smiled through the day, I was so tired and too weak to even enjoy it to the fullest.

We had a lovely picnic together and I had an hour out of the wheelchair which was also nice to spread my legs out on the grass.

Mum packed us some home made scones and some special iced biscuits. I love how she managed to ice our initials onto them. :)

Bless her.x

November 15th

I've asked Karl to move the mirrors from my room.

I can't stand to see myself each morning, I look and feel awful with bones sticking out where I didn't know I had them.

Karl says he loves me just the same as he's always done, bald and bony as I am but I can't love myself right now, not looking like this so I'd rather not have that reminder every time I wake up.

Sarah has been trying her best, bless her, helping me with makeup and hair stuff but it's just not the same me that I'm looking at anymore. It's a stranger who has had some alien thing take over my body.

It's getting harder and harder to get this diary out written in and then hidden again so I may miss some days, sorry...I will try my best.

Good night...x

November 19th

Today the reality of this illness hit me hard big time and I needed to write my feelings down.

We had a call from Brad in Miami today to say that Marie passed away in her sleep last night.

He said it was peaceful for her thank goodness but it really hit me hard. I know it won't be too long until...until my time comes and everyone is crying for me. I really don't want them to hurt.

Karl had to go outside after the call and I know he was crying although he said he wasn't when he came back inside. He tried to be so brave, especially in front of the children.

They said we can attend the funeral through a video link which will be nice, sort of. At least we can be there in some way.
I really feel for their children and it brings it all home as to what our two will be going through when the inevitable happens to me.

Oh man...please let them be strong, please be strong my beautiful babies. :(

I've been thinking about the hospice that Paula mentioned so many months ago now and thinking that maybe it's time for me to book in before Christmas is upon us. I will have to chat to Karl about it in the next few weeks and get him to sort something out. He seemed to be pleased with the whole place when we visited.

I know he will probably want to care for me himself here but it's not fair to give him that amount of responsibility and I know how hard it gets closer to the end.

Goodnight dear diary. Xx

November 23rd

Sarah helped me look for a few bits of Christmas shopping online.

I wanted to get the kids some bits just in case I'm not able to in the next few weeks but nothing seemed to stand out for me.

What do you get your kids at a time like this?

Nothing is going to make up for the way I'm making everyone feel.

It's supposed to be the best time of the year but I feel like I'm ruining it for them.

Again...I hate you Cancer!

I hate you for taking me away from my family and I hate you for causing them to be so upset.
I see such sadness in their eyes when they look at me and my stupid bald head and gaunt face.

Where has the energetic, fun mum gone? I've gone somewhere very dark and very boring and it's not nice.

Be strong woman - that's what I keep telling myself, be strong for them, for Karl, for mum, for Sarah.xx

Jane.xx

December 1st

I decided to talk to Karl this evening about going into the hospice.

He was running me a lovely bubble bath to soak in after another tiring day doing...well, nothing because I don't have the bloody energy. :(

I think he wanted to talk me out of it but I am thinking this is the best thing to do at the moment for the family.

I'm hoping it's not a mistake and that they will forgive me for not wanting to be at home but I just feel so terrible having them deal with all the medicine, the washing, cleaning of me as well as the house. I can't seem to just admit defeat and let them do everything.

It's for the best isn't it?

Here are the questions again.???

J...xxx

December 2nd

So, Karl called the hospice when he'd settled me in the lounge so I could watch the children decorating the outside trees with some Christmas decorations.

I'm booked in. I'm going to the hospice this evening.

Hopefully, things will be easier for Karl and the kids if I'm there so I'll try and write when I can.

I'm watching my children throw some tinsel on the trees outside and it's pretty much carnage but I love it so much. They've dug out some of the older baubles from the christmas box to hang out there too. I suppose when Karl puts some lights around it all it will look better but I don't care how it looks.

I just love seeing them having fun with it and even when they start arguing about who puts what where! It's funny to me and makes me smile so it's all good.

I'll miss seeing their display at home but maybe they can do something at the hospice for me too.

xx

Night night..xx J xx

December 4th

It's been a few days since I came here and I guess it's okay but...it's just not home.

I don't know what else or how else I was expected to feel I suppose - it's not home but it's the best place for me, isn't it?

There I go again asking myself questions in a diary which doesn't answer back???

I've got to try and deal with it.

It's best for me to be here where everything is done and the equipment, drugs, nurses and care are amazing.

Karl is coming in again soon with the kids and mum. Can't wait to see them.

I told Karl to take the kids to the cinema last night so they could have a bit of normal time out from here and the sadness of it all.

I can't remember what they said they were going to see but no doubt, I will get all the info in a bit.

Going to have a quick nap before they come so signing off for now.
x Jane x

December 6th

I've been really trying to stay smiling about being here but it's so hard.

The staff are beyond incredible but I just feel like I wasn't supposed to end it here.

I'm having such a sad day today and when mum came in this morning, all I seemed to do was cry.

I felt bad for her having to see me like that. I could see in her eyes she has been devastated by this, by me being so ill and being so upset today.

Tomorrow, I will be stronger - I WILL!!!
Xxx

*Note to self: Be stronger for everyone.

Be strong Jane - I tell myself again and again.

J

December 9th

It's been a few days since I've written because I've just not known what to write to be honest.

This place is nice but it's not home.

I thought it would be my final place but I'm not happy here and I want to go back to my house - my home.

I'm not unhappy with the care or anything like that - they are all just amazing and deserve medals for what they do. I just, I just want to be at home.

I don't know if I can face Christmas in this little room so I'm going to ask Karl to take me back home when he comes in.

I'm laying here alone listening to nothing but silence or someone crying and it's just getting too much.

Tomorrow, I've decided, I'm going home!

That is where I want to end my life - in my beautiful house. :(
xxx

J xx

December 10th

I'm home. :)

I love my family so much for doing this.

Karl carried me out of the hospice like the hero he is and I'm so thankful to him and the staff there for understanding my need to do this.

My bed feels so nice. :)

Maybe I'll get to see Christmas after all???

Who knows?? I suppose only you know don't you...Cancer, you know when don't you???

On the way home, the most beautiful thing happened and something that no-one else knows about. (Not unless this diary is found after I'm gone). Something I probably will never get the chance to speak about so I wanted to record it here for my own reasons.

Maybe I will get time to read all this back and remember how bloody lucky I was, in the scale of things.

What happened? ...I saw James - that's what bloody

happened!

I saw him one last time at the cemetery and it was almost, kind of, well...magical - he was just there one second and then gone at the blink of an eye, we saw each other one last time - and I feel as though we said goodbye for good.

I felt bad for thinking he was a little weird when we first met, well not weird but...oh I don't know. I just know that he was there for me at one of the worst times of my life and no matter how or where he came from and why, I am so grateful and will treasure those times we had laughing and joking around, chatting mostly and being there for each other I guess.

Maybe I'll see him on the other side??

I'm so tired now - it's even hard to write these days

Bye for now.
xx

December 11th

I got Karl to just talk to me about memories we had over the years last night but I think I may have fallen asleep while he kept talking. His voice is so soothing to my ears these days, like he whispers so as to not cause me any more pain than I'm already in, bless him.

Sarah came in this morning with a big bunch of flowers from Carol and the crew at work. I think they looked even more beautiful than ever. Maybe things are just looking sharper for me these days. Maybe I'm just seeing things in a different light.

I don't know, everything seems prettier now that I've got more time to look at them I guess.

I don't know.???

Strange things are happening in my mind now, strange things like James? Still not over that I guess.

The flowers had a note with them telling me about Perry and the fact that his baby had arrived earlier than expected.

He's named her Courtney-Jane. :)

This made me emotional, how lovely of him to add my name.

What a cute guy.

I've told Sarah about the letters and where to find them, she's promised me she will do it for me but only at the right time. They can't have them before.

This is probably my last entry in here now so here's one last boost of pen energy to leave this year on.

I can't manage to add anymore entries in here, one because I have to keep trying to reach for it stuffed under my mattress without anyone finding it and another, well, it's just hard.

Hard to write, hard to express my constant anger and sadness etc etc..:(

I feel so weak today and if I'm truly honest with myself, I think I'm almost ready to go, I think it's time to go.

I feel like I just want to go to sleep now, you know, for good.

I'm too tired to fight this thing anymore.

As much as I want to see Christmas, I don't think it's going to happen.

It's even hard to hold my pen, so, this is it...I guess it's my last diary day.

Goodbye diary, goodbye to me...xxx J xxx

Notes:

Some extra notes I'm pre-writing for my beautiful family incase I can't write near the end:

If any of my family finds this diary after I'm gone, please know that I loved you with all my heart for as long as I could and I am so sorry for lying to you.

I just wanted to try and protect you from the hurt, the sadness and the pain that I was feeling during the early part of all this.

Please believe me when I say I'm sorry, I'm sorry, I'm so so sorry a million times over.

Don't be upset, don't be sad for me, be strong...for me, please be strong.

Kids - be strong for dad. xx

Goodbye to you all - I love you more than anything.

Love Jane,
(mum, wife, best friend, daughter) - loved being them all.
xXx

About The Author

T.a. Rosewood

Traci, who writes under the pen name, T.A. Rosewood, wrote her first short story when she was just thirteen years old, which was called, Looks Aren't Everything.

During a GCSE English exam, she had to write a two-page short story, but, once she'd started writing, she ended up with a thirty-page document and was graded down for that English exam. That story was called 'The Runaway', a young adult story.

During her twenties, Traci began writing poetry and has been published in five different poetry collection books. Unfortunately, she had to stop writing as her working life and family grew.

Almost two decades later, in 2016, she was inspired to write again, when she met bestselling author Jojo Moyes at the open evening of Harts Books in Saffron Walden, Essex.

Traci and her husband went along to show their support for the new book shop in town and listened intently as Jojo Moyes described how it felt when her bestselling book Me Before You was turned into a Hollywood Film.

At that moment, Traci turned to her husband and said: "I'm going to start writing again."

That evening, she couldn't sleep for excitement and come up with a fictional storyline for Reasonable Lies, which would highlight a sensitive women's health issue.

Sadly, one month into writing her novel, Traci's mum, was diagnosed with the same disease as the lead character in Reasonable Lies, which put an immediate stop to her writing, as it was just too painful to continue.

Thankfully, after two operations and eighteen months of treatment, her mum was given the all-clear, and she then encouraged Traci to continue with writing her book using her as research and inspiration.

In October of 2019, Traci and her Husband, Leonardo, attended the Harts Books 'Meet the Author' Event, to hear Jojo Moyes talk about her latest book, The Giver of Stars.

During the 'Ask the Author' anything section, Leonardo raised his hand to thank both Jojo Moyes and Harts Books, and further explained how Traci had been inspired to write her debut novel from Jojo's first visit to the store.

JoJo congratulated her and started to applaud, which then lead to a round of applause from the rest of the audience.

This impactful evening kick-started lots of follows on social media, requests from local book clubs wanting to read Traci's book, and subsequently, lots of pre-orders for her first book, Reasonable Lies which was published in March 2020 on Amazon.

Now, this diary has been released which is a short follow up to Reasonable Lies.

Traci lives in North Essex with her husband, family, and two westies.

Praise For Author

If you've read Reasonable Lies then this next follow-up book is for you.

Jane's Journal is written as diary entries and is a perfect accompaniment to Reasonable Lies. So many times I have read books and wanted to know more about the Main Character and this really hits the spot.

The book was so easy to read, I felt as though Jane was talking directly to me.

- DANIELLE, BOOK REVIEWER.

Oh my goodness. I felt guilty reading it as if I'd stolen someone's real diary and was reading their innermost thoughts and feelings. It's an excellent complement to the original book.

Oh how I cried and cried (the emotional incontinent

I am)! The author writes with such compassion and feeling and that just bursts off of those pages and straight into your heart. I loved it.!

Oh…..and I'd buy a box of tissues while you're at the shops as well!!

- LYN, BOOK REVIEWER

What can I say other than @tarosewood has done it again.

Jane's Journal is the perfect accompaniment to Reasonable Lies.

I was lucky enough to be sent a draft to read and let me tell you, it was like I was actually reading a diary (some points I generally forgot it was just a book). It's such a brilliant way to connect with Jane, it might be crazy to say but it made me feel closer to her. (Yes, I know she's fictional)

Much like the main book, it brought all the emotions (tissues definitely recommended).

- ABBIE, BOOK REVIEWER

I have been one of the lucky ones to have read this before it's available for sale (see Amazon soon!)
The one thing that it left me with was wondering how Jane had lied to all her family - this book gave me those answers.

The journal delves into Jane's thoughts and feelings about it all which for me explained a lot more about why she did it. It made me empathise with her even more. It also made me cry all over again!

A must read for after Reasonable Lies ▢ a ✫✫✫✫✫ from me!

Roll on more books from this wonderful author...

- CLAIRE, BOOK REVIEWER

Books By This Author

Reasonable Lies

Acknowledgement

Big thanks to my husband for this
idea of Jane's personal diary.

Thank you to all those who read the draft
for me and encouraged me to release it.

Read & Review

If you enjoyed this little book, please leave a review on Amazon for me - it really helps us self-published authors to reach even more readers.

All you have to do is add a few comments and voila!

Thank you so much for reading.

You can keep up to date with all my new books, news, book signings and much more through the following:

www.tarosewood.com
instagram.com/tarosewood
facebook.com/tarosewood
twitter.com/tarosewood

Printed in Great Britain
by Amazon